EARLY EXPERI

If Thomas Alva performed *all* the experiments in the book he must have performed one so dangerous that it should never be attempted except under the watchful eye of a trained adult scientist. Perhaps Al was wise enough not to fill a little cardboard house with hydrogen gas and to touch it off with a spark of electricity. He might have burned the Edison home to the ground. Some such event at about this time, however, aroused his mother's concern. Nancy did not like the popping sounds she heard from the basement, nor did she like some of the smells, particularly when Al was experimenting with sulphur. So she put her foot down firmly, telling her son to "clean out the whole mess."

Al pleaded tearfully for his precious laboratory. His mother finally weakened, insisting, however, that he promise never to try a really dangerous experiment. She also insisted that all the poisonous chemicals be labeled. Al gladly complied. On each of 200 bottles he lettered POISON, adding a skull and crossbones. *He* knew the actual contents of each bottle, but the warning would serve to keep meddlers from touching his treasured chemicals.

YOUNG
THOMAS
EDISON

STERLING NORTH

PUFFIN BOOKS

PUFFIN BOOKS
Published by the Penguin Group
Penguin Young Readers Group,
345 Hudson Street, New York, New York 10014, U.S.A.
Penguin Group (Canada), 90 Eglinton Avenue East, Suite 700, Toronto,
Ontario, Canada M4P 2Y3 (a division of Pearson Penguin Canada Inc.)
Penguin Books Ltd, 80 Strand, London WC2R 0RL, England
Penguin Ireland, 25 St Stephen's Green, Dublin 2, Ireland
(a division of Penguin Books Ltd)
Penguin Group (Australia), 250 Camberwell Road, Camberwell, Victoria 3124,
Australia (a division of Pearson Australia Group Pty Ltd)
Penguin Books India Pvt Ltd, 11 Community Centre, Panchsheel Park,
New Delhi - 110 017, India
Penguin Group (NZ), 67 Apollo Drive, Rosedale, North Shore 0632,
Auckland, New Zealand (a division of Pearson New Zealand Ltd)
Penguin Books (South Africa) (Pty) Ltd, 24 Sturdee Avenue, Rosebank,
Johannesburg 2196, South Africa

Registered Offices: Penguin Books Ltd, 80 Strand, London WC2R 0RL, England

First published in the United States of America by Houghton Mifflin Company Boston,
The Riverside Press Cambridge, 1958
Published by Puffin Books, a division of Penguin Young Readers Group, 2009

1 3 5 7 9 10 8 6 4 2

Copyright © Sterling North, 1958
All rights reserved

THE LIBRARY OF CONGRESS CATALOG CARD NUMBER: 58-9637

Puffin Books ISBN 978-0-14-241210-7

Printed in the United States of America

For
Arielle, Ole, and Little Randy,
with the love of the author

AUTHOR'S NOTE

In *Young Thomas Edison*, I have striven to bring back to life the inventor of the phonograph, the incandescent light, and motion pictures. Edison was one of the most human individuals who ever saved a child's life, roared with laughter over an amusing story, lost a fortune without bitterness, or courted his bride-to-be by tapping his message of love in the Morse code. Sharp-tongued and tender, whimsical and grim, playful and serious, his genius was only one side of his complex humanity. If I have made him live and breathe again for my young readers, I shall be satisfied.

I am particularly indebted to the staff of the Edison Laboratory National Monument of West Orange, New Jersey, for assistance in checking the scientific and historical aspects of this book. I wish to thank Melvin J. Weig, Superintendent, for suggesting the book in the first place, and for tireless labors in its behalf. I also wish to thank Norman Speiden and Harold Anderson, Curators of the museum, for their meticulous reading of the manuscript. If any minor error still remains, it is the fault of the author and not of the Edison Laboratory.

Sterling North

CONTENTS

LET THERE BE LIGHT

When the wires go down in a big storm we are suddenly aware of an earlier, darker world—the world before Edison perfected his incandescent light. We grope through the gloom with candles, our shadows looming large upon the wall.

It is as though the house were dead. No button or switch or dial responds to our touch. The television set is silent and dark. The little motors in our many household appliances refuse to turn. Refrigerators and freezers soon cease to be cold. Electric stoves and percolators and toasters give no heat. We huddle around the fireplace like cabin dwellers, aware that even the oil burner in the furnace cannot operate without its electric oil pump.

For a day or two this primitive existence is high adventure. But it is hard to keep clean without hot water. We strain our eyes trying to read by flickering yellow light. Soon we tire of this strenuous game of playing we are pioneers. It takes most of our energy merely to survive.

During thousands of years the human race lived among such shadows—dim caves, dim hovels, dim castles, damp and cold. No wonder so many tribes worshiped the sun—lit torches, lamps, or candles at every festivity! Light is precious and hard to obtain, and darkness breeds fear, ignorance, and superstition. We step back centuries when the lights go off. And how grateful we are when those incandescent globes begin to glow again.

When Thomas Alva Edison died in 1931 at the age of eighty-four, he had more than one thousand inventions to his credit, including such miraculous ones as the phonograph and moving pictures. Of all his contributions to mankind, however, his greatest was his perfection of the electric bulb—inexpensive, odorless, and dependable—light in such abundance that no monarch of the past could even imagine such luxury.

We are children of light! Without the sun's warm and cheerful rays, we would swiftly die. Without electric light and power we would slowly slip back into a world of shadows. We honor the light-bringers of this world—those who seek to banish ignorance and darkness. And this is the principal reason why Thomas Alva Edison has become one of the America's most authentic heroes. He was a bringer of light!

⌒ 1 ⌒
THE COCOON
UNFOLDING

"Suppose . . . we show to the child . . . the cocoon un-folding, the butterfly actually emerging. The knowledge which comes from the actual seeing is worth while."
Thomas A. Edison

Even though it is the shortest month in the year, February has reason to be proud. It has given to America George Washington, Abraham Lincoln, and Thomas Alva Edison.

A blizzard was sweeping across Lake Erie on the midnight of which we are speaking. Drifts were piling deep around the brick cottage of Samuel and Nancy Edison in the village of Milan, Ohio. Now oil lamps began to glow through the frosted window-panes, and blue smoke swirled upward from the chimneys of the little house. A teen-age son, William Pitt Edison, was silhouetted for a moment in the lighted doorway, bundled warmly for his mission. Then the door was banged shut by the wind, and the boy plunged into the storm to bring Dr. Leman Galpin—much needed at the Edison cottage on this particular night.

The cause of all this excitement was a new baby, soon to be christened Thomas Alva Edison. His arrival at three in the morning on the eleventh day of February, 1847, was characteristic of the strange hours he was to keep throughout most of his life. The baby was "fair with gray eyes, and the very image of his mother. He seldom cried."

There in the little back bedroom of the cottage, tired Nancy lay beside her seventh child. Did she know the old superstition that a seventh offspring sometimes becomes a wonder-working wizard? Certainly this baby's large and well-shaped head suggested intelligence—or so Nancy hoped, looking down fondly at her new infant.

Little Thomas Alva, known throughout his boyhood as "Al," seems to have inherited much of his appearance and intelligence from Nancy Elliott Edison, the bright and pretty schoolteacher Samuel had married nineteen years before. Now at the age of thirty-seven, Nancy still retained some of her early beauty, the blue-gray eyes and chestnut hair, plus a smile both warm and wise.

Samuel Edison, a robust man of forty-three, looked down from his towering height upon his wife and newest child. His hair and beard were silver, and there was always a twinkle of merriment around his eyes. Although Thomas Alva would at first seem frail, eventually he would become a man of iron endurance—his father's son in this respect at least.

On Nancy's side of the family the blood was mostly Scots. On Samuel's side it was largely Dutch.

As far back as the male line can be traced,* the Edisons were vigorous, outspoken men who lived to a ripe old age. Usually they reared good-sized families of lively children. Samuel and Nancy got off to an excellent start in this respect, having, in fairly

---

*Family tradition insists that the Edisons crossed the stormy Atlantic from Holland in the year 1730 to settle on a large farm in New Jersey (not far from the spot where, 160 years later, Edison would build his great laboratories in the Orange Mountains).

Thomas Alva's *great-grandfather* was a Tory sympathizer named John. After the American Revolution he was forced to flee to Nova Scotia. Thomas Alva's *grandfather* was another high-spirited man. His name was Samuel and he became a captain in the Canadian forces during the War of 1812. Thomas Alva's *father* was also named Samuel. In the year 1828 he married Nancy Elliott, a descendant of Ebenezer Elliott, who had been a captain in Washington's army.

swift succession, three healthy babies—Marion, William Pitt, and Harriett Ann (known throughout life as "Tannie"). The family operated a clean little hotel in Vienna, Ontario; and here they might have spent their lives had not Samuel, like his grandfather before him, decided to risk his future by backing an unpopular and dangerous cause.

In the late 1830's, a number of discontented Canadians staged a small rebellion, something like our own American Revolution, but completely unsuccessful.

When the rebellion was crushed, almost before it had started, Samuel became a hunted man. He had to flee for his life—or at least for his liberty. Traveling night and day in bitter weather, he dashed nearly one hundred miles through the snowy wilderness to the St. Clair River, where he crossed the international border into the newly formed state of Michigan. Here on United States soil he was safe from capture.

In due time Samuel Edison found a likely place of residence in the thriving little grain port of Milan, Ohio. Here he began the profitable manufacture of wooden shingles. One of his best friends was a ship's captain named Alva Bradley. Captain Bradley was happy to be the messenger who brought the good news to Nancy and her children that a new home had been prepared for them in Ohio. Shortly thereafter she crossed Lake Erie on Bradley's sailing ship, bringing the children and the household goods.

Three more babies were born between the arrival of Tannie and the advent of Thomas Alva. All three died as infants. The names on the little gravestones were Carlisle, Samuel, and Eliza. No wonder Nancy Edison felt fiercely protective toward her seventh and final child.

Thomas Alva's first memory was that of chasing a Mexican silver coin—perhaps a half dollar—across the golden locust-wood floors of the cottage in Milan. The coin was tossed there for his amusement by a prosperous farmer named Homer Page, who had come courting Al's oldest sister, Marion.

His next memory was that of being held in someone's arms as Marion in her wedding gown stood beside Mr. Page to take her marriage vows. He distinctly remembered hearing her say, "I do!"

His third memory was of several covered wagons, brightly painted and roofed with white canvas, which stopped for the night near the Edison home. Here were whole families with all their worldly goods, heading through Indian country toward the far gold fields of fabled California. Around the campfires the bearded men and sunbonneted women sang "Oh, Susannah" and boasted of the fortunes they would make, once they had crossed the arid plains and the terrible mountains.

"This was my first impression of a great world beyond," Edison later recalled. He had a tremendous yearning to "climb into those prairie schooners—just to see where they were going. Gold didn't mean a thing on earth to me—in fact it hasn't meant much to me all my life. But I did want to know where those wagons went when they disappeared down the road."

Eighteen forty-seven was an interesting year in which to be born. Through a peaceful settlement with England, and through war with Mexico, the United States was adding a far-western empire as large as the original Thirteen Colonies.

The steam engine, harnessed to the paddle wheels of steamers and to the drive wheels of locomotives, propelled more and more of the nation's passengers and freight. For the moment the canals were prosperous, but the railroads, pushing ever westward, would soon acquire most of their traffic. Wherever the iron tracks were laid, the wires of Samuel Morse's newly invented telegraph were sure to go.

In Chicago, Cyrus Hall McCormick had built a factory to mass-produce his famous grain reapers. Everywhere one might see the crude beginnings of mechanization. Thus was the stage prepared for the arrival of Thomas Alva Edison, one of the greatest inventors of all time.

Concerning all this early ferment of invention and expansion little Thomas Alva at first knew almost nothing. All around him, however, lay tantalizing clues; and from a very early age this bright boy showed a strong desire to mend his ignorance. He reasoned that the way to learn is to explore, experiment, and ask questions.

His explorations began with excursions along the towpath of the canal that lay at the foot of the bluff—a fascinating ribbon of water wide and deep enough to float Lake Erie grain boats of 250 tons. The canal had been in operation for eighteen years when Al was born. Its principal freight consisted of hundreds of thousands of bushels of Ohio-grown wheat, brought into Milan in huge wagons drawn by six-horse teams. As many as 300 wagons a day slanted down the hill past the Edison cottage to discharge their golden cargoes into the grain elevators along the canal. Frequently, between dawn and dark, twenty boats would ascend the canal from Lake Erie to load that same wheat for further transportation.

These boats were mostly barges and sailing vessels, some of them built on the canal in Milan. When a vessel was launched from the shipyards of Mr. Merry and Mr. Gay it was indeed a Merry and Gay occasion, with half the town standing on the bluff and cheering.

It was an easy scramble from the Edison back yard down the hill to the towpath and canal where the mules walked briskly, pulling the ships and barges. From the sailors, mule drivers, and lumberjacks, Al learned dozens of songs and ballads, not all of which he dared to sing at home.

Naturally this active boy sometimes fell into the canal—as did every other boy in town. Of course he was rescued and switched with the willow branch Nancy Edison always kept for this purpose behind the old Seth Thomas clock. Al's yearning for adventure never wavered, however. Once, high in a grain elevator, he fell into the wheat and would have been smothered had not strong arms pulled him swiftly to safety.

Edison is reported to have been somewhat frail and sickly in his infancy. Frail or not, he was one of the most active small boys in Milan, visiting every sawmill, gristmill, and other business establishment in the village. One day, even before he knew his ABCs, he was found on the town square laboriously copying the store signs on his slate. He would stop occasionally to tug his right eyebrow, a lifelong habit when he was puzzled. Then he would begin again, methodically attempting to draw the letters.

His early experiments included sitting for hours on a nest of goose eggs to see if he could make them hatch. With scrap lumber from one of the sawmills he constructed little plank roads and bridges. While trying to dig out a nest of bumblebees he was bunted by an angry ram. Life was continuously exciting.

Al was as curious as a chipmunk, and as bursting with energy. At the shipyards, where he carefully examined every tool, he asked the workmen so many questions that he became something of a nuisance.

He asked his mother, his father, and all the neighbors questions, too!

Where does the wind come from?

How high up are the stars?

His well-shaped head was one big question mark. Neighbors, noticing his large head, sometimes murmured, "Brain fever." They thought that any child who asked so many questions must be "queer." Besides, they did not always know the answers.

"Well, *why* don't you know?" he asked.

The boy was obviously strange. Even his father was a trifle worried. Edison's mother knew her son, however.

"Leave him alone," she said, "Al knows what he's about."

Al's only experience with school was brief and painful. Under a man named Engle and his wife, who ran a small tuition school, he spent three miserable months always at the "foot of the class." The scholars ranged from children smaller than Al to big hulking boys and girls of eighteen or more, all crowded into one noisy room. The Engles had little patience with Al, whose mind seemed far away as he drew pictures on his slate. Exasperated with the youngest

Edison, and completely unaware of his potential talent, they sent him home in tears.

"My teachers say I'm addled," Al told his mother sadly.

Nancy was furious. Taking her son by the hand, she marched to the schoolhouse and gave the Engles a scolding they would not soon forget.

"This boy is brighter than you are," she said. Unlike many tiger mothers who have made similar claims, Nancy was right.

All this was still in the future, however, and in another town to which the Edisons soon would move.

Here in Milan, the neighbors had long suspected that Al was "addled." What could one say for the intelligence of a boy who insisted that wood and iron should be able to "talk"?

How could these scornful neighbors know that eventually Thomas Alva Edison would make wood, iron, and wax not only talk, but sing whole operas and play entire symphonies? How could they know that the little boy next door would one day become the inventor of the miraculous phonograph?

Milan was a village that blossomed like a flower and then as swiftly faded. The canal was the stem of that flower, nourishing its growth. When the canal started to decline, the town no longer flourished.

What had happened was this: the town fathers of Milan had invested their money in the canal, and for a quarter of a century their investment seemed secure. When a railroad company offered them a proposition which would have brought the railroad to Milan, they refused to co-operate, believing still in their canal. The railroad went instead to a nearby town, which soon captured all the grain traffic.

Fewer songs were now heard along the towpath, and fewer ships came gliding up that quiet ribbon of water. One grain elevator after another was boarded up. Soon the village square was all but deserted on Saturday night. Many citizens were leaving Milan.

Obviously the time had come for a change of address, and luckily the Edisons had saved enough money for the move. Little Al did not grieve. He was always ready for new adventure.

2

THE YOUNG EXPLORER

*"We can derive the most satisfying
kind of joy from thinking
and thinking and thinking."*

Thomas A. Edison

If you will glance at a map of Michigan you will see that Detroit lies between Lake Huron and Lake Erie on the waterway connecting these two lakes. Now run your finger north and a trifle east to the point where Lake Huron empties into the St. Clair River. Here you will find Port Huron, the destination of the Edison family when they moved—lock, stock, and barrel—in 1854.

Father, Mother, and three Edison children were aboard the little steamer *Ruby* when she made her first run up the river that spring. Samuel Edison and his wife Nancy were aging a bit, but still sturdy and hopeful. Their daughter, Miss Tannie, who liked to write verses, was as quaintly attractive as any picture in *Godey's Lady's Book.* Standing beside her at the rail was her brother William Pitt, old enough to vote and showing so much talent with pencil and paintbrush that his father and mother sometimes talked of sending him to Paris for art lessons. Most active and vocal of the Edisons was seven-year-old Thomas Alva, bright-eyed with the excitement of this voyage.

Of these three Edison children, Thomas Alva alone was fated for fame. William Pitt would operate a livery stable, and later the street railways of Port Huron, his art only a pastime. Tannie would spend her adult life as Mrs. Samuel Bailey. But the alert small boy now visiting the engine room, now dashing through the salon, or standing at the prow with the spring wind blowing his always unruly hair was destined to a more significant future.

You may be certain that Al asked many questions of his mother and father as the *Ruby* breasted the strong current, its engine throbbing. Now that the ice was out, the river was busy with traffic. The shrill whistle of the *Ruby* saluted grain boats and lumber boats, side-wheelers, and schooners. Now and then a birchbark canoe glided by, loaded deep with pelts of beaver, mink, and fox—a harvest of valuable fur from the winter's trapping. To the rhythm of the canoe paddles, there sometimes drifted across the water the melody of a *voyageur*'s ballad, reminding the passengers on the *Ruby* that the French were the explorers who had first come this way.

Darkness had fallen before the little steamer reached Port Huron. Thomas Alva, tired from his long and exciting day, was sleeping soundly. He awoke next morning sharing a bed with his big brother in a Port Huron hotel. Soon the entire family was on its way to their new home just north of that town—a gracious Colonial house with a wide center hall, four large fireplaces, and six big bedrooms upstairs. The ceilings were high. Many windows gave light to the well-proportioned rooms. Wide porches, front and rear, furnished shade and comfort during the warmer months.

Below ground was the dry and cavernous cellar for storing barrels of Michigan potatoes and bushels of apples, carrots, beets, and cabbages, plus many shelves of pickles and preserves. Here also was space for what would presently become young Edison's first experimental laboratory.

This "House in the Grove" had once been the home of the prosperous trader who had furnished supplies to nearby Fort Gratiot—a military strong point which had been used intermittently for more than a century and a half, first by the French, and since 1814 by the United States Army. In fact even now, on the military parade ground lying north of the house, soldiers sometimes trained and marched.

To the west stretched the almost unbroken forest, a source of great lumber wealth. To the south, toward Port Huron, lay a pleasant triangular grove of oaks and pines. Most exciting of all was the view to the east, where, not far from the house, the swift, ice-cold St. Clair River curved by, pouring endlessly from blue-green Lake Huron only a mile upstream.

Across the river lay the Canadian town of Sarnia. Not far downstream, Al's father had fled across this international boundary seventeen years before. It had been this part of Michigan which had welcomed him to safety. No wonder he had brought his family to prosperous and friendly Port Huron when business in Milan had slackened. Already Samuel Edison was organizing the feed and grain business which would support his family in their new location.

The Edisons had reason to be pleased with their new home with its orchard, its big garden, its old plantings of lilacs and other shrubs and flowers.

There was a stable for keeping horses and a cow if they so desired. Overhead, wild ducks and Canada geese were wedging northward toward their Arctic nesting grounds. When Samuel asked his wife if she liked her new home, she glanced up with her warm, quick smile.

In later years it always amused Edison to tell of his earliest and most childish experiments. He was a good storyteller and perhaps he improved his tales for the sake of artistry. However, being an honest man, he never seriously altered the facts.

At an early age he became convinced that human beings should be able to fly. The method he used to give wings to mankind might have encouraged neighbors in their belief that Al was addled.

Balloons rise because they are filled with a gas lighter than air. Among the chemicals and drugs which Al had gathered in the basement was a big bottle of effervescent Seidlitz powder—a popular medicine of the period, and obviously an excellent source of gas lighter than air. Al was too shrewd to try the experiment on himself. Looking about for a victim, his eye lit upon his adoring friend, Michael Oates, the

Dutch boy-of-all-work around the Edison home. Mike would do almost anything for Al, whom he rightly considered the smartest boy in Port Huron.

However, Mike was suspicious when Thomas Alva offered him an oversized dose of Seidlitz powder. Fly? Who wanted to fly? And besides, how could he ever get down if he started floating upward toward the clouds?

Al told him to grab the branches of the tree above him as he soared by. He would later be rescued with a ladder.

Shutting his eyes, Mike dutifully downed the enormous dose. Then he waved his arms as he had been told. But Mike showed no talent whatsoever for flying. Instead he soon lay groaning on the ground.

This time Nancy Edison used her willow switch in earnest. There were to be no more flying experiments around the Edison household. Al was persuaded that it might be wise to turn his talents in other directions.

Edison's mother had been trained as a schoolteacher. She now had for a pupil a boy much brighter than any she had previously instructed. Using the books that were at hand, she soon taught Al not only how to read words, but how to read and understand serious history.

The Edisons had a remarkably good library for a family of that period and region. Among their other books were several many-volume sets, including: Sears' *History of the World,* Hume's *History of England,* and Gibbon's *The History of the Decline and Fall of the Roman Empire.* Before he reached the age of twelve, Edison, with the help of his mother, had read all these books and many others. Samuel Edison aided the process by giving his son twenty-five cents for each book read.

Because of his native intelligence and his mother's teaching ability, Al managed to master college-level history when most boys of his age were still spelling their way through *McGuffey's Fourth Reader.*

Edison was later of the opinion that the average mind begins to wither between the ages of eleven and fourteen. Unless young people use their brains to full capacity, they may find that their thinking machinery has "rusted." Edison contended that non-use of the brain is like non-use of the body. Put your arm in a sling for a few weeks and you find it is so weak you can scarcely lift it. In just the same way, the lazy-minded soon become mental invalids.

Edison never made the fatal mistake of mental laziness. Whether he was reading or experimenting, his brain was as active as the lithe body of an open-field runner or a figure skater. His mind was always healthfully aglow.

Naturally he was fascinated by Gibbon's masterpiece, *The Decline and Fall of the Roman Empire,* the brilliant and readable account of the Goths and Visigoths and Vandals sweeping down upon the luxury-loving Romans, who had been weakened by years of self-indulgence and soft living. How much Edison actually digested from Gibbon's 3000 pages devoted to fourteen complicated, action-packed centuries, we shall never know. But undoubtedly his mother drove home the moral that pride and sloth come before destruction, and that young and vital tribes will always be a menace to old, decaying cultures.

Edison and his mother did very well with most of the books they tackled. But they failed completely when they tried to read Sir Isaac Newton's *Mathematical Principles of Natural Philosophy.* In fact, Edison never did become a good mathematician. Today, in our much more complicated world, mastery of higher mathematics is absolutely essential to success in any technological field—a truth that

Edison himself realized when he helped devise the questions for the Edison Scholarship tests.

Although he failed to master Newton, Al nevertheless preferred science to any other subject. He spent many happy hours studying Richard Green Parker's *School Compendium of Natural and Experimental Philosophy*, an introduction to physics and several other sciences (as those subjects were known in the 1850's). Al not only read the book, he performed every experiment in it, refusing to trust the author's findings until he had tested each one himself.

Thomas Alva's laboratory in the basement was becoming a place of magic. From the ash piles of Port Huron, he and Michael Oates had gathered medicine bottles, liquor bottles, old glass Mason jars, in fact any glass receptacle that would hold a powder or a liquid. Into these containers Al had put every chemical he could afford to buy, plus many easily obtained substances such as cornpith, milkweed fibers, salt, sugar, and flour.

Parker's *School Compendium* was exactly the right text for a young experimenter. It showed Al how to construct a crude barometer to test atmospheric pressure. Now he knew in advance when to expect a storm. It taught him the basic laws of mechanics, which allow man to lift or move huge weights. Using small levers, pulleys, wheels, inclined planes and wedges, Edison himself could test these laws.

From this wonderful little book Edison learned about our fiery sun and all its circling planets. Here too were facts about those distant suns we call the stars, which every night spread their glory above the "House in the Grove" and over the darkly gleaming river.

Page after fascinating page told him of the wonders of the world around him: how light is affected by passing through lenses; how sound travels through the air, through water and through solids. Al learned how water turns a waterwheel; how air can be compressed; and how a pump can be made which will create a vacuum.

Best of all were the three chapters on electricity and magnetism. Here Edison learned for the first time how to generate electricity by petting a cat, or by rubbing a glass rod with silk. By whirling a copper disc between two poles of a horseshoe magnet he could manufacture a continuous current just as Faraday did when he invented this simple generator in 1831.

Like Alessandro Volta (the Italian physicist who died in 1827), Al made a battery. Using a piece of zinc for one pole and a piece of copper for another, he immersed these electrodes in a dilute acid. The result was a feeble but dependable electric current.

Two of the most exciting pages in the whole book concerned the telegraph, a new invention introduced by Professor S. F. B. Morse. The author ranked this invention with the "greatest ever achieved." And here, for the first time, Edison found the Morse code alphabet consisting of dots and dashes—the thrilling new secret language of the electric wire.

If Thomas Alva performed *all* the experiments in the book he must have performed one so dangerous that it should never be attempted except under the watchful eye of a trained adult scientist. Perhaps Al was wise enough not to fill a little cardboard house with hydrogen gas and to touch it off with a spark of electricity. He might have burned the Edison home to the ground. Some such event at about this time, however, aroused his mother's concern. Nancy did not like the popping sounds she heard from the basement, nor did she like some of the smells, particularly when Al was experimenting with sulphur. So she put her foot down firmly, telling her son to "clean out the whole mess."

Al pleaded tearfully for his precious laboratory. His mother finally weakened, insisting, however, that he promise never to try a really dangerous experiment. She also insisted that all the poisonous chemicals be labeled. Al gladly complied. On each of 200 bottles he lettered POISON, adding a skull and crossbones. *He* knew the actual contents of each bottle, but the warning would serve to keep meddlers from touching his treasured chemicals.

One sentence in Parker must have set Edison dreaming: "Man has as yet but lifted the veil, behind which the stupendous operations of nature are carried on. What wonders he will discover, should he penetrate the recesses of her laboratory."

Then as now, there were wonders still to be discovered, unimaginable wonders. A seed had been planted in a bright boy's brain which eventually would flower into some of the greatest inventions of all time. Young Thomas Alva Edison had begun the lifelong process of mastering the secrets of our magnificent universe.

When Thomas Alva wasn't underground in his laboratory, he was often above the treetops on the platform of his father's observation tower, scanning the landscape through an old telescope that was mounted on the tower. There was no better place in the world to play pirate, or to read a book, or merely to gaze out upon wave-swept Lake Huron and the eddying river.

This observation post, more than 100 feet above the ground, was called "Edison's Tower of Babel" by the amused neighbors. The tower was typical of the restless, adventuresome Samuel Edison, who in his fifties was still busy with new projects—not all of them practical. Al's father had built this tower hoping to make a fortune from picnickers who, he believed, would pay twenty-five cents each to climb this gently swaying structure to view the landscape. In the first few weeks of operation he had exactly three paying customers. Eventually, however, the tower did pay its way, attracting on one gala occasion 600 excursionists on a single day.

One "customer" who never complained about the dizzy height was Al, who every day raced up the swaying steps to look out over his little kingdom of river, lake, and forest.

Like his father, Thomas Alva had many ideas for making money. The family provided food, clothing, and shelter, but chemicals and experimental apparatus were expensive. For instance, the equipment needed to conduct the experiments in Parker's *School Compendium* is listed in the book, and is priced at a total of $260. Since the value of the dollar was much greater during the 1850's than it is today, Al's economic problems were serious.

At the age of eleven Thomas Alva and his friend Michael Oates raised ten acres of vegetables in the field beside the house. They plowed, dragged, planted, hoed, and harvested, simmering under the summer sun. Then with a horse and wagon they peddled their fresh, attractive vegetables through the streets of Port Huron and other nearby towns. Presumably the boys were allowed to keep some small part of their hard-earned money. However, Al is said to have turned over to his mother in a single season the then vast sum of $600.

Still short of cash for laboratory equipment, and somewhat weary of "hoeing corn in a hot sun," Al looked around for better employment. An opportunity quickly presented itself. In Edison's own words:

> The Grand Trunk Railroad was extended from Toronto to Port Huron, at the foot of Lake Huron, and thence to Detroit, at about the same time the War of the Rebellion [the Civil War] broke out. By a great amount of persistence I got permission from my mother to go on the local train as a newsboy. The train from Port Huron to Detroit, a distance of sixty-three miles, left at 7 A.M. and arrived again at 9:30 P.M.

In other words, Edison, a boy in his early teens, made a round trip each day which took fourteen and one-half hours, including several hours in the bustling city of Detroit. Al made good use of those hours. It took him but a short time to buy the fruit, candy, nuts, newspapers, and magazines he needed for peddling on the train. The rest of his afternoon was largely spent in the Detroit library. Edison later wrote, "I started, it now seems to me, with the first book on the bottom shelf and went through the lot, one by one. I didn't read a few books, I read the library."

Al's long and busy day was not enough to consume his entire energy. When his father would allow it, he stayed up half the night reading and experimenting. He believed then, and for the rest of his life, that "grit, determination and hard work" can make a success of almost any young man. He never ceased to test that theory to the utmost of his endurance.

"After being on the train for several months," Edison recalled, "I started two stores in Port Huron—one for periodicals, and the other for vegetables, butter and berries . . . These were attended by two boys who shared in the profits . . . After the railroad had been opened a short time, they put on an express which left Detroit in the morning and returned in the evening. I received permission to put a newsboy on this train . . . in addition [I] bought butter from the farmers and an immense amount of blackberries in the season . . . As the war progressed the daily newspaper sales became very profitable, and I gave up the vegetable store."

One would think that a boy busy all day on the Grain Trunk Railway, employing at least three other boys, and attempting to read the entire Detroit library would consider his time occupied; but such was not the case.

With the help of a friend named George Pullman (who later became famous as a builder of sleeping cars) he installed a "rolling laboratory" aboard the train, complete with racks of bottles, vials, and beakers. With the permission of the train authorities, Al occupied an unused part of the baggage car for his experiments. Unfortunately, among his chemicals was a highly inflammable stick of phosphorus immersed in water, and this phosphorus would eventually create serious trouble for the boy. Meanwhile Al was happy. As the little mixed train with its passenger and freight cars puffed and tooted down the uneven tracks to Detroit, young Edison, between trips through the cars shouting his wares, continued his experiments.

Then one day in a stationery store in Detroit, Al saw a most desirable and exciting piece of machinery. It was a secondhand printing press, complete with type. Immediately the young businessman realized its value. Why not install it in the baggage car? There he could write, set in type and print a weekly newspaper filled with gossip and news, of interest not only to passengers but to citizens of Port Huron, Mount Clemens, and the other towns along the line. Al was friendly with all the telegraphers. He was certain that they would help him to pick up news "hot off the wire."

The fact that he had no experience as a reporter and must learn how to hand-set the type did not give Al a moment's hesitation. He was certain that with application he could learn to do anything.

A photograph of this ambitious boy taken at about this time—in his fourteenth or fifteenth year— shows him in a jaunty dark cap, gray trousers, dark wool coat, and hand-knit muffler. There is an amiable grin on his strong and rather handsome face. No one riding the local was better liked than this would-be journalist now entering the publishing profession.

Only one or two copies of the *Weekly Herald* have survived, and these are priceless collectors' items. When it was being published by Al Edison, however, the paper sold for three cents a copy, or, by subscription, eight cents a month. In a very short time, 400 customers were buying each issue of the paper, and it was netting him more than a dollar a day—a good wage in those times for a full-grown laborer. This furnished Thomas Alva the dollar that he paid his mother each day for his board and room. Now everything he earned from his many other businesses became clear profit which could be used to purchase more chemicals and laboratory apparatus.

The *Weekly Herald* was "the first newspaper ever published on a moving train." It is said to have attracted favorable comment not only in Detroit, but as far away as London. It made Al mildly famous in his part of Michigan. Considering his age and lack of formal schooling, the paper was remarkably newsworthy, bright, and well edited. Young Edison already knew that human interest sells newspapers, and his little publication was crammed with human interest.

Editing his own paper was merely a sideline. Al's real business on the train and at stations along the way was selling a large number of other newspapers and periodicals. In addition to paper-backed novels, he peddled *Harper's Weekly, Harper's Monthly, The Saturday Evening Post,* and two or three hundred copies each day of the Detroit *Free Press.*

A vital but troubled nation, tragically split over the issue of slavery, created more than enough news to keep the newspapers smoldering when Edison was a boy. This continuous clash of regional interests may have been good for newspaper circulation, but the endless struggle was anything but good for national unity.

In the short decade and a half since Thomas Alva had been born, anger had flared with increasing intensity both in the North and in the South. Now with the outbreak of the Civil War thousands of luckless boys and men were expressing with bullets and cannon balls the anger previously expressed only in words.

There must have been a difference of opinion in the Edison household at Port Huron at about this time. Samuel Edison was a Southern sympathizer— sometimes an outspoken one. Once again he was taking an unpopular political stand despite all possible consequences. But Sam's older son, William Pitt, was so firm for the Union that he left his new wife and baby to volunteer in Lincoln's growing army. Al was too young to go, but from many of the items in the *Herald* one can feel his sympathy for the Northern cause.

As we have said, the intense excitement about the war created a great demand for papers, and Edison soon learned to judge his probable sales from the nature of the headlines. On the sixth of April, 1862, while waiting around the circulation department of the *Free Press* in Detroit, Al read the first bulletins concerning the ferocious Battle of Shiloh. General Ulysses S. Grant, in charge of strong Northern forces, had been caught partially unprepared by the Confederates. Wild rumors suggested that the total casualties for both armies might rise to 60,000 or more. And still the battle raged.

Realizing that this was the most serious clash of the war to date, Edison decided he could sell 1,000 rather than his usual 200 or 300 papers. To buy such a large number, he needed credit. The man in charge of circulation thought Al was "crazy" and refused to give him such a huge supply. But Wilbur F. Storey, the crusading editor of the paper, grinned when he heard the request and scribbled an enabling message, which Edison gratefully preserved to the end of his life.

With the help of other boys, Edison carried his 1,000 papers to the train. Then he laid his plans carefully. As he would later tell the story:

> All along the line I had made friends of the station agents, who were also the telegraphers . . . They were a good-natured lot . . . and had been kind to me. I wired ahead to them, through the courtesy of the Detroit agent . . . asking them to post notices

that when the train arrived I would have newspapers with details of the great battle.

When I got to the first station on the run, I found that the device had worked beyond my expectations . . . After one look at that crowd I raised the price from five cents to ten and sold as many papers as the crowd could absorb. At Mount Clemens, the next station, I raised the price from ten cents to fifteen . . . By the time the train reached Port Huron I had advanced the price of the Detroit *Free Press* for that day to thirty-five cents per copy, and everybody took one.

Out of this one idea I made enough money to give me a chance to learn telegraphy . . . something I long had wished to do.

Thomas Alva was rather certain that he could handle any job on the Grand Trunk line, including that of engineer in the cab of the locomotive. One evening he had a chance to test his self-assurance.

The engineer and the fireman had been celebrating on the previous evening and were very drowsy. Edison, who was riding in the cab, offered to take the throttle for the last thirty miles of the run into Port Huron. He was a bright boy who had often observed the engineer at work. He knew how to advance the throttle, toot the whistle, and ring the bell. He also knew that the boiler must never be allowed to run dry. But on several other matters he was slightly vague.

While the engineer and fireman slept peacefully, young Edison drove the beautifully polished engine, pulling its handsomely enameled cars, northward over the flimsy Grand Trunk tracks toward Port Huron. The novice engineer brought the train successfully to its various stops with only a few neck-spraining jolts. He was equally successful in getting under way. At one water tank he filled the boiler to the brim, complimenting himself on his thoughtfulness.

Then on a straightway where it seemed safe, Al decided to try for a little speed. Notch by notch he advanced the throttle. With his head out the window and the wind in his hair, he felt the thrill of the increasing pace. Suddenly from the stack there erupted a geyser of hot black mud which gushed over the beautiful brasswork of the engine and plastered wet, greasy soot all over the brightly painted cars. Al slackened his speed, wiped the stinging mud from his eyes, and proceeded with more caution.

At another stop, Thomas Alva remembered that

here was where the engineer always walked out to oil the steam chamber. However, when Al opened the oil vent, the blast of steam nearly knocked him to the ground. Closing the vent with difficulty, he climbed back into the cab, hoping he could reach Port Huron without additional oil. This he accomplished. But once again in the final miles, black mud cascaded like lava from a volcano as the engine "blew its stack."

With a sigh of relief young Edison brought the train into the Port Huron station, where the station agent and the now awakened engineer and fireman laughed loudly at the boy. They explained that he had put so much water in the boiler it had overflowed into the smokestack, loosening the soot and creating a real Vesuvius. They also explained that in oiling the steam chamber one must first turn off the steam.

In telling this story, Edison always criticized himself for having been so previously unobservant—a lesson he thoroughly learned on that memorable evening. It is typical that he was self-critical, and failed even to mention the irresponsibility of an engineer so drowsy that he could not run his locomotive.

It is a wonder that Thomas Alva Edison ever survived to become a world benefactor. Frequently he jumped from the train before it came to a full stop, or leaped aboard after it was moving. On one such occasion the results were tragic. Al ran along the platform and tried to climb into the baggage car, but the train was rolling so rapidly that he could not pull himself aboard. He hung on for dear life and might well have fallen under the wheels had not one of the trainmen lifted him "by the ears" into the car. Edison heard something "snap" in each ear, and the pain for a time was intense. "Earache came first, then a little deafness, and this deafness increased until . . . I could hear only a few words now and then."

Even though he never regained his hearing, Edison could tell of his loss philosophically when he was mature and famous. However, the quiet world must have seemed depressing to an active, ambitious boy, eager to see and hear everything in the exciting universe around him. When a grown man, he once remarked that he hadn't heard a bird sing since he was a boy.

Often on the train these days a customer would speak twice to the young news vender before he was understood. At home when the family gathered at the table, Al was often accused of paying no attention when he was addressed. They thought his mind was elsewhere—lost in his books or in his countless laboratory experiments. As yet, no one suspected the real cause for his inattention.

Despite this new complication in his life, Thomas Alva continued to be an active, good-natured, and slightly mischievous boy who loved to play a practical joke if he saw no harm in it.

At Fort Gratiot, raw recruits were being trained for the Union Army. This camp was hundreds of miles north of the battle lines, and was, of course, in no danger of attack. Nevertheless, to give these soldiers practice, sentries were posted in a picket line around the fort, and were ordered to keep watch during the night. The men on sentry duty were spaced at considerable intervals and could communicate only by shouting. For instance, if they wanted the corporal for some urgent reason, a picket would shout, "Corporal of the Guard!" The next picket would take up the cry, and the next, until finally the fat little corporal came running and panting to discover the cause of the excitement.

This whole performance struck Al as immensely

amusing. So with the admiring Michael Oates, he decided to play a trick on the picket line and the corporal. Creeping stealthily into a thicket north of the house, the boys awaited the perfect moment. Then Al shouted through the gathering darkness, "Corporal of the Guard." All up the picket line went the resounding cry, and soon the plump little corporal was panting down the path, seeking the cause of the disturbance. Much angry and bewildered conversation ensued as sentry after sentry denied any knowledge of the reason for the call. Al and Michael smothered their desire to howl with laughter.

This had been so successful that the pranksters could scarcely wait to try it on a second night. Again the results were madly gratifying. But the third time they tried it, matters went differently. The evening seemed unnaturally silent as they crept to their hiding place. There was no *tramp, tramp* of heavy shoes along the path.

Al was about to shout "Corporal of the Guard," when soldiers sprang up everywhere. As Edison later recalled it, they caught Michael Oates and ". . . took him to the lock-up at the fort . . . They chased me to the house. I rushed for the cellar . . . there were two barrels of potatoes and a third one, nearly empty. I poured these remnants into the other barrels, sat down, and pulled the barrel over my head, bottom up. The soldiers had awakened my father, and they were searching for me with candles and lanterns. The corporal was absolutely certain I came into the cellar, and couldn't see how I could have gotten out, and wanted to know from my father if there was no secret hiding place . . . I was glad when they left, as I was cramped, and the potatoes were rotten that had been in the barrel and violently offensive."

Edison waited until all was quiet in the big house, then climbed stealthily up to his bed. There his father found him in the morning, just after Michael Oates had been released from the guardhouse. Never before had Samuel Edison switched his son—a duty left for his mother to perform. However, this time he ordered Thomas Alva to get out of bed, and gave him "a good switching on the legs."

Al was too big to cry. He walked over to the window, his legs smarting, and looked out on the scene of his fairly innocent crime. Samuel asked him if he had learned his lesson, but the boy did not reply. His father spoke more sharply, and Al turned, slowly.

"Did you say something, Father?"

Quite suddenly Samuel Edison realized that his

son was deaf. He never punished Al again, and one can only hope that Nancy, too, less seldom used the "switch behind the old Seth Thomas clock that had the bark worn off."

Although Thomas Alva was taken to local doctors, none could aid him. The damage to his ears seemed permanent. In later years, Edison claimed that the loss of his hearing was a positive benefit. It gave him a blissfully silent world in which to concentrate on his inventing and his reading; it shut out "small talk," idle chatter at the table, and the noise of the great cities.

"The things I have needed to hear I have heard," Edison explained. He felt that his nerves were better for the silence in which he lived. When a great ear specialist told the inventor that he could improve his hearing, Edison refused to be aided. He preferred his quiet world, free from the "uproar of civilization."

Nevertheless, we may be sure that no such mature philosophy softened his loss when he was a boy, deprived of the whisper of the wind through the pines and the songs of the birds on an April morning.

A second misfortune endangered Al Edison's

happiness at about this time. One evening when the train was puffing northward over a stretch of particularly rough track about ten miles from Port Huron, the stick of phosphorus fell from its container in the "rolling laboratory" and immediately broke into flame. In a matter of seconds the dry wooden floor of the baggage car was ablaze. Al tried his desperate best to put out the fire, but it seemed a losing battle.

When Conductor Stephenson saw what had happened, he rushed into action, extinguishing the blaze with the fire buckets. Little damage had been done to the car, but the conductor was furious with the boy. There would be no more such "nonsense" on his train. At the very next station, which happened to be Smith's Creek, he pushed Al, his printing press and his laboratory off the train, breaking some of the precious equipment. And there the youngster stood, as near to tears as he would permit himself—his broken world in ruins all around him—supperless and miles from home on the dark platform of the Smith's Creek station.

3

WANDERING TELEGRAPHER

*"From the start I found that deafness was
an advantage to a telegrapher. While I could hear
unerringly the loud ticking of the instrument,
I could not hear other and perhaps distracting sounds.
I could not even hear the instrument of the man
next to me in a big office. I became rather well-known
as a fast operator, especially at receiving."*

Thomas A. Edison

On a morning in August, in the year 1862, while
Edison was still making his daily trip to Detroit, an
event occurred which helped to shape his future. The
busy little locomotive which pulled the mixed train
had a second duty to perform. At each station it
stopped long enough to switch freight cars before
continuing its run.

While Al waited on the platform at Mount Clemens on this hot August day, a freight car rolling

down the siding suddenly endangered Jimmy Mackenzie, the station master's three-year-old son, who
was playing with pebbles between the rails.

Al tossed aside his bundle of papers and made a
running dive for the child, carrying him out of harm's
way by a matter of seconds. Neither was hurt, although the big boy and the little one sprawled in the
gravel, bruising their hands. Then Thomas Alva carried the frightened Jimmy to his father and mother,
who remained grateful to Edison for the rest of their
lives.

The station agent, J. U. Mackenzie, was a rela-
tively poor man. He could not reward Al with money,
even had the boy been willing to accept it. He offered
instead a far greater reward, an opportunity to learn
telegraphy. Naturally Al was delighted.

(How did the sale of those 1,000 papers head-
lining the Battle of Shiloh help Edison to master the
art of the telegraph key? Probably by giving him a
comfortable nest egg of savings—enough to pay his
board bill at home for weeks to come. Now he could
spend most of his time learning his new profession.)

As we have seen, Al was not completely unknowing on the subject of telegraphy. For several years he
had been trying to solve mysteries that even Parker

didn't explain concerning this means of communication. Once he asked a line repairman exactly how the messages were sent over the wire. The Scotsman told him laughingly that the telegraph was like a very long dog. When you pulled its tail in one city, it barked in another.

Thomas Alva, of course, was not satisfied with this explanation. So he continued to experiment.

With the aid of another boy, James Clancy, he built a ramshackle homemade telegraph line which extended for half a mile between the Edison house and the Clancy cabin in the woods. The boys used stovepipe wire. This was attached to trees, fence posts, and makeshift telegraph poles, which swayed in the wind. For insulators they used the necks of glass bottles. Electric current was supplied from a wet-cell battery, also fashioned by the young experimenters.

Both boys had a rudimentary knowledge of the Morse code. On a memorable occasion, they had the great joy of tapping out slowly a few words over the stovepipe wire. When Telegrapher Clancy couldn't understand Telegrapher Edison he would step outside his cabin and, using a megaphone, shout at the top of his lungs, "What did you say?"

Every evening the boys sent messages, then entire

news stories, but at a painfully halting pace, quite unacceptable for professional sending and receiving. In time a wandering cow that had jumped the pasture fence ran into the telegraph line and spent the night becoming increasingly entangled. So great was the wreckage of broken poles and twisted wire, that the Edison-Clancy line never was put back into operation.

Now at Mount Clemens, Al had a chance for professional coaching from his friend Mackenzie. Mrs. Mackenzie's daily contribution was a good, hot dinner. Al spent long and happy hours at the telegraph key experiencing the thrill of sending paid messages to Detroit and more distant places. Soon he was mastering many tricks of the trade.

Later in Port Huron, Al set up a small telegraph office, operating first from a drugstore, and later from a combination jewelry-and-book store. However, business was slow, messages few, and the total income very limited. Young Edison spent much of his time experimenting, reading, and tinkering with small inventions. Then came a crisis which demonstrated his remarkable ability.

When ice swirled down the St. Clair River breaking the underwater cable, all telegraphic communication between Port Huron and Sarnia, Ontario, was destroyed. To splice the cable in such weather was all but impossible. Al, however, conceived a temporary remedy. Borrowing an old engine from the Grand Trunk, he sent the Morse code by piercing blasts of the locomotive whistle. Interested spectators gathered on the other shore, and very soon the operator in Sarnia solved the riddle. He too borrowed a locomotive to toot messages in reply.

Doubtless such exploits aided Al's reputation along the Grand Trunk railroad. They may have helped Mackenzie line up for his young friend a job at Stratford Junction, Ontario, where Tom Edison (as he now signed himself) began his four years as a wandering telegrapher.

Edison's job at Stratford Junction was that of night telegraph operator at a salary of $25 a month. During the daylight hours he conducted his usual experiments. Naturally he found it hard to stay awake at night.

Like all the other operators along the line, Tom was supposed to check in every hour with the signal "six" to assure the chief dispatcher in Toronto that he was awake and on the job. He did this faithfully for a time, then devised a method for getting more sleep at night. His convenient little invention consisted of a notched wheel, so attached to a clock that punctually on the hour the clever little gadget would tap the necessary signal on the telegraph key, while Edison slept happily on, dreaming of his inventions. Eventually the chief dispatcher caught him at this trick and reprimanded him severely. Tom now stayed awake and sent the signal himself.

Edison was not drowsing on the night the near-accident occurred. In fact, he was blameless in an episode which, nevertheless, cost the young man his job. Warned to stop a freight to let another train from the opposite direction pass, Tom wired his OK, and rushed to the platform, where no signalman was to be found. He dashed back to wire the dispatcher to hold the other train. However the dispatcher, trusting that Tom had signaled the freight, had given the go-ahead to the second train. Again Tom rushed to the platform, only to see the freight roaring by, unaware of its danger. Two locomotives dashing toward a head-on collision! What could be done?

Running after the freight in the forlorn hope that

he might somehow prevent the wreck, Tom stumbled in the dark, fell into a deep ditch, and was knocked unconscious.

Meanwhile, both engineers were very much on the job. Each saw the terrifying sight of an oncoming headlight flashing down that single track. Both managed to bring their locomotives to a stop a few feet from mutual destruction.

Tom was called to Toronto, where the general manager of the Grand Trunk was threatening dismissal as the mildest penalty. While the young telegrapher sat trembling in the outer office, two visitors from England arrived to see the general manager. Taking advantage of this brief respite, Tom slipped away, boarded a freight, and eight hours later was on the ferry from Sarnia to Port Huron. Edison never did try to collect his final month's wages from the Grand Trunk.

Even a seventeen-year-old, dismissed from his last employment, could acquire another job at the telegraph key during those Civil War years. Many of the seasoned telegraphers, both in the Confederacy and in the Northern states, were at the front, assisting in this new kind of war—a conflict directed largely by telegraph and supplied largely by railroads.

Edison was soon at work at Lenawee Junction near Adrian, Michigan. Not long after, he drifted on to Fort Wayne, Indiana, and then to Indianapolis.

All the "plug" operators in those days wanted to become first-class "lightning slingers," fast enough on the receiving end to take the press copy for the newspapers which came streaming over the wires, mostly at night. Tom, wearing his always untidy clothes, living in a hall bedroom, and spending every cent he earned on chemicals, laboratory apparatus and books, not only worked as a "plug" operator all day, but also volunteered to substitute at night whenever a regular night operator failed to appear, which was frequently.

Press copy on these nights came in too fast for Tom and for another telegrapher named Parmalee. But Edison was equal to the occasion. As he told the story in later years:

I got two old Morse registers and arranged them in such a way that by running a strip of paper through them, the dots and dashes were recorded on it by the first instrument, as fast as they were delivered from the Cincinnati end, and were transcribed to us through the other instrument at any desired rate of speed or slowness. They would come in on one instrument at the rate of fifty words a minute, and we would grind them out the other at the rate of twenty-five. Then weren't we proud! Our copy used to be so clean and beautiful that we hung it up on exhibition; and our manager used to come and gaze at it in silence with a puzzled expression. Then he would depart shaking his head . . . He could not understand it; neither could any of the other operators; for we used to drag off my impromptu automatic recorder and hide it when our toil was over.

Pride, however, comes before a fall. On a November evening in 1864, when the election returns were fairly flooding the wires, showing that Lincoln had been reelected for another term as President over General McClellan, not even the help of the automatic recorder could save Edison and Parmalee. Said Edison: "Copy kept pouring in at the top rate of speed, until we fell an hour and a half or two hours behind. The newspapers sent in frantic complaints, an investigation was made, and our little scheme was discovered. We couldn't use it any more."

Seventeen-year-old Tom Edison, still a "plug" tele-grapher for all his native brilliance, had here the germ of an idea which in time would become his automatic repeating telegraph. Little did his manager realize that this young "tramp telegrapher" would go down in history with Galvani, Volta, Davy, Faraday and Professor Morse himself—a genius of the very first order in all matters electrical and telegraphic.

In Cincinnati, where he next appeared, Edison swiftly increased his skill as a telegrapher. He had just turned eighteen when he arrived at this city on the banks of the Ohio River, and it was here that he won advance-ment from $60 a month as a plug to $125 a month as an ace operator, able to take messages as fast as anyone could send them. Tom was in Cincinnati when Lee surrendered to Grant at Appomattox, thus ending the Civil War—a tremendous story coming in over the wire and sending a great wave of joy sweep-ing over all the Northern states. But that joy was soon cut short by another message, equally historic, which was taken down by one of the Cincinnati op-erators so automatically that it made no impression on his mind. Learning of the news, a crowd in the street began shouting, "Lincoln is dead! Lincoln has been shot!"

"Who took that message?" asked the grim manager of the Cincinnati telegraph office.

One of the operators (not Edison) bowed his head in sorrow and shame. He had taken down the words without so much as realizing their meaning.

Edison's best friend in Cincinnati was a restless, romantic, devil-may-care, wandering telegrapher named Milton F. Adams, who took pity on the younger man who seemed so shabby and alone in this new town. Milt took him to see Shakespeare's *Othello,* a play they both admired. Sometimes they would listen to the music of a German band. When both left this city, Adams moved northward and eastward, finally landing in Boston. The Civil War over, Edison thought he would like to see the South. He was an operator in Nashville until early 1866. Then he went to Memphis, where his swiftness at the key during an interstate competition earned him the proud title of "Champion of the Mississippi Valley." But still he went without decent clothes, even without an overcoat, to have money to buy chemicals and books.

It was in Memphis that he progressed much further in his improvement of the automatic recording device which had been so useful in Indianapolis. In this instance his brilliance cost him his job.

"At that time," he recalled, "a message sent from New Orleans to New York had to be taken at Memphis, retelegraphed to Louisville, taken down again by the operator there, and telegraphed to another center, and so on until it reached New York. Time was lost and the chance of error was increased. I was the first person to connect New Orleans and New York directly. It was just after the war when I did this. I perfected my repeater, which was put on at Memphis and worked without a hitch. The manager of the office . . . had a relative who was also busy on the same problem, but I got in ahead of him and received complimentary notices in the local papers. This made the manager mad and he sent for me the next day.

"'You have been making a disturbance in the operating room and you are discharged,' he said.

"'But—' I began, conscious of innocence; and there he interrupted me. 'Don't argue,' he said, 'just . . . get out.'"

As was usual with Edison, he was almost completely without funds. He and another operator in the same predicament managed to travel a short distance on a limited railroad pass. Then they were put off the train and had to walk 150 miles to Nashville with only a dollar or two between them. For protection from the cold, they had only their ink-stained linen dusters. All around them snowstorms swirled and bitter winds blew. From Nashville they obtained a railroad pass to Louisville, where they arrived in the midst of yet another blizzard. Said Edison: "I shall never forget the sensation we made in that city walking through the snow in our airy apparel."

Edison worked longer in Louisville than in any other Middle Western city during these vagabond years. It was here that he developed through experimentation his beautiful script, the fastest form of writing for him, and so neat and legible that it looks like copperplate. In this combination of printing and script, he could take up to fifty-five words a minute from the telegraph wire to the delight of newspapermen awaiting this press copy. Another talent of Edison's made him popular with the press. An electrical "leak" in the cable under the Ohio River garbled as much as twenty per cent of all the incoming messages. To fill in these scrambled gaps in every message,

Edison made it his business to read every paper he could obtain. He was so well informed on all the big stories that he could usually guess or invent the missing phrases. Only once did he mistake the meaning of an important news story, for which he was not very severely scolded.

Edison interrupted his Louisville stint with a trip to New Orleans. Here he and two friends seriously considered trying their luck in South America. Fortunately an old Spaniard convinced Tom that the United States, not Brazil, was the great land of the future. Tom did not sail. His two friends, who ignored the good advice, soon died of yellow fever in the tropics.

Back in Louisville once more, Edison's passion for experimenting again led him into trouble. One night he needed acid from the battery room. He tipped over a carboy of the liquid, which went through the floor and all over the manager's desk in the room below. Once again he was on his way.

He served a brief second term of employment in Cincinnati. Then, at the request of his aging mother, he visited his parents in Port Huron. They had come upon hard times and were living much more humbly than when they had owned the gracious Colonial house at Fort Gratiot. Tom realized that if he was ever going to help them, he had better start making his fortune promptly. Perhaps the East would offer greater opportunities.

Tom wrote his friend Milt Adams, now in Boston. Milt showed Tom's letter to the manager of the Boston telegraph office. The manager was impressed, more by the beautiful script than by Tom's stated qualifications. He said that if Edison could take messages in a hand such as that, he could have a job.

As poorly dressed as he had been during all his wandering years, and still using a linen duster for an overcoat, Tom started for Boston in sub-zero weather. The Grand Trunk passenger train on which he was crossing eastern Canada became stalled in a blizzard for three days. Passengers much more warmly dressed than Edison came near to freezing to death. The thermometer registered twenty-eight degrees below zero, and Tom, like all the other male passengers on the train, worked for long hours shoveling snow. Finally the track was clear enough for the engine to plow ahead through the drifts; it arrived four days late in Montreal.

Boston, with its proper Bostonians and its air of

culture and wealth, did not faze Tom Edison. He arrived in that city looking more like a tramp than an ace telegrapher or an upcoming inventor. Despite his odd and shabby appearance he was immediately put to work in the Boston telegraph office, on a wire from New York.

"I sat down unsuspiciously at the table," Edison recalled, "and the New York man started slowly. Soon he increased his speed, to which I easily adapted my pace. This put my rival on his mettle, and he put on his best powers . . . At this point I happened to look up, and saw the operators all looking over my shoulder, with their faces shining with fun and excitement."

This was obviously a put-up job. They had purposely given Edison the fastest man in New York, and they were waiting to see him "break," but Tom was not easily bested. Calmly he dashed off the flying message in his perfect script, meanwhile pretending that this was nothing but routine telegraphy.

"The New York man then commenced to slur over his words, running them together and sticking the signals; but I had been used to this style of telegraphy in taking report, and was not in the least discomfited. Finally, when I thought the fun had gone far enough

. . . I quietly opened the key and remarked, telegraphically, to my New York friend: 'Say, young man, change off and send with your other foot.'"

Edison had passed the test with colors flying. The quiet office burst into an uproar of happy congratulation, and the odd-looking boy from the Middle West became something of a hero to his Boston office mates, who never again played a practical joke on him. They knew a great telegrapher when they met one.

Edison and Milt Adams were like brothers during this Boston period. They roomed together, haunted the bookshops together, and shared the same quiet pleasures they had enjoyed in Cincinnati. One day while they were browsing in a bookstore Edison came across a complete set of the works of Michael Faraday, the great English chemist and physicist, whose pioneer work in electricity had always fascinated him. Tom bought the entire set and became wildly impatient to get it home to their poor room so that he could begin reading it. Hour after hour he kept his eyes glued to the pages, refusing to sleep and barely willing to eat. Milt Adams finally lured him to breakfast, which they ate at a place a mile distant from their room.

Milt later said, "Edison's brain was on fire with what he had read, and he suddenly remarked to me: 'Adams, I have got so much to do and life is so short that I am going to hustle,' and with that he started on a run for breakfast."

Hustle he did for the rest of his action-packed, thought-packed life, frequently working, reading, and inventing twenty hours out of each twenty-four. He was now twenty-one years of age. He thought he might live to be fifty. How could he possibly do all that he dreamed of doing unless he labored night and day the year around, holidays included?

Meanwhile Edison was working on his first invention acceptable to the United States Patent Office, the vote recorder, which he hoped would save thousands of precious hours in every legislative assembly in the world. But he was inventing without knowledge of the delaying tactics which are the stock in trade of politicians everywhere. Of this first and futile invention he later wrote:

My first appearance at the Patent Office was with an ingenious contrivance which I called the Electric Vote Recorder. I had been struck with the enormous waste of time in Congress and the State legislatures by the taking of votes on any motion . . . so

I made a plan . . . In front of each member of the House were two buttons, one for "aye" and one for "no." By the side of the speaker's desk was erected a square frame . . . When the vote was called for, each member pressed one or another of the buttons in front of him, and the number of "ayes" and "noes" . . . at once appeared automatically on the record.

Edison was certain that his fortune was assured. However, when he demonstrated his device in Washington to an influential member of Congress who might have helped its adoption, that worthy said to Tom, "'Young man, that won't do at all. That is just what we do *not* want. Your invention would destroy the only hope the minority would have of influencing legislation. It would deliver them over bound hand and foot to the majority.'

"I saw the force of his remarks," said Edison, "and was about as much crushed as it was possible to be at my age."

This was in 1868, when Edison was twenty-one. This early defeat did not turn him away from inventing, but it did inspire in him the resolve never again to perfect an invention that was not widely desired by the world at large.

4

FIRST FRUITS
OF VICTORY

*"Show me a thoroughly satisfied man—
and I will show you a failure."*

Thomas A. Edison

Late in the year 1868, Edison announced that he had
"resigned his situation in the Western Union office,
Boston," and would "devote his time to bringing out
his inventions."

Early in 1869 he borrowed enough money to pay
his fare on the night boat from Boston to New York,
and arrived in America's greatest city on a cold winter
morning, ill-clad, hungry, and without a cent in his
pocket. On that first morning in New York he saw a
tea taster at work in the window of a warehouse.
Stepping inside, he asked this kindly man if he might
have a cup of tea. That was his entire breakfast.

In those days following the Civil War, when the
value of paper money fluctuated wildly, many speculators thought that the safest form of wealth was

gold. In some of the larger cities there were gold exchanges and therefore the need for swift reporting on the rapidly changing market value of the yellow metal. In Boston, Edison had set up a telegraphic service (with forty private subscribers) continuously reporting on the price of gold. This venture proved to be an inventive success but a business failure.

It was quite natural that when he arrived in New York he should go to the offices of a similar company (though a far more successful one), operated by Dr. S. S. Laws, inventor of the Gold Reporting Telegraph. Laws' device had dials that telegraphically registered the price of gold. The system was operated from a central office, speeding its information over wires to each of the 300 subscribers.

For three days and nights while he awaited employment, Edison haunted this central office of the Laws concern, sleeping in the basement battery room, and spending every waking hour studying the master instrument that sent out the messages. Then a most fortunate misfortune occurred. But let Edison tell the story:

"On the third day of my arrival, and while sitting in the office, the complicated general instrument . . . suddenly came to a stop with a crash. Within two minutes over three hundred boys—a boy from every broker in the street—rushed upstairs . . . all yelling that such and such a broker's wire was out of order and to fix it at once. It was pandemonium, and the man in charge became so excited that he lost control of all the knowledge he ever had."

One can imagine the panic in Wall Street. Fortunes could be made or lost in a very short time on the rapidly changing price of gold. Brokers and speculators were desperate, and Dr. Laws' whole gold-reporting service was threatened with collapse.

But to continue with Edison's quiet version of the story: "I went to the indicator, and, having studied it thoroughly, knew where the trouble ought to be, and found it. One of the innumerable contact springs had broken off and had fallen down between the two gear wheels and stopped the instrument; but it was not very noticeable . . . Dr. Laws appeared on the scene, the most excited person . . . I ventured to say that I knew what the trouble was, and he said, 'Fix it! Fix it! Be quick!'"

Edison soon had the machine working smoothly again. Dr. Laws was grateful and interested. He asked Tom his name and also how much he knew about the gold-reporting system. Edison was soon explaining to the amazed inventor how he could improve and simplify his machine. This so impressed Dr. Laws that he offered to put Tom in charge of the entire plant at the unbelievable salary of $300 a month. Said Edison when telling this story:

"Three hundred per month! This was such a violent jump from anything I had ever seen before, that it rather paralyzed me for a while . . . but I determined to try and live up to that salary if twenty hours a day of hard work would do it. I . . . made many improvements, devised several stock tickers."

From "rags to riches" in three days is quite a success story even for a genius such as Edison. But the deeper meaning was that for years he had been preparing for just such a moment. This time opportunity was knocking at the right door.

Compared to today's well-regulated market for buying and selling stocks and bonds, Wall Street in the 1860's, '70's, and '80's was a wild and woolly free-for-all with no holds barred. Jay Gould and Jim Fisk were but two of the more spectacular "robber barons" and shrewd manipulators. Their corner on gold threw Wall Street into a short but desperate panic on Black Friday (September 24, 1869). One banker went crazy. Dozens were suddenly bankrupt.

Tom could congratulate himself that what few dollars he had saved had not been risked in this wild speculation.

After a few months Edison and Franklin L. Pope, a highly intelligent telegraph engineer, founded a concern of their own called Pope, Edison and Company, with J. N. Ashley as a third and silent partner. This was the first firm of electrical engineers ever established, and the young technicians promised to perform almost any miracle one might ask in the realm of electricity.

In the *Telegrapher* they bought advertising space to announce that they would design special telegraphic and electrical instruments, carefully and reliably test "Instruments, Wires, Cables, Batteries, Magnets, etc.," and would prepare "Claims, Drawings and Specifications for Patents." These ambitious engineers were prepared to construct, reconstruct, and maintain private and commercial telegraph lines and would install "Fire-Alarms, Thermo-Alarms, Burglar-Alarms." Moreover they would act as purchasing agent for: "Telegraph Wires, Cables, Instruments, Insulators, Scientific and Electrical and Electro-Medical Apparatus," or almost anything else you might care to name.

Pope and Edison blazed the trail to an exciting new profession. But the going was difficult at their little shop. Operating without any capital except their unlimited optimism, this small concern bravely launched yet another telegraph service for the purpose of giving quotations on the price of gold and sterling.

The Gold and Stock Telegraph Company which had recently bought out Dr. Laws now acquired Pope, Edison for a nominal sum. General Marshall Lefferts, president of this much bigger company, was well aware that the real asset was Edison himself. He set the young inventor to work, urging him to produce a simple, foolproof stock ticker. Edison was happy with his new assignment and threw himself into the task.

For the first time in his life Tom had a little money, and his thoughts turned to his father and mother. An affectionate letter written at this time is still to be seen at the Edison Institute in Dearborn, Michigan. Edison had heard that his mother was not well and that his father was having to work very hard.

"I guess you had better take it easy after this," the son says with affectionate concern. "Don't do any hard work, and get mother anything she desires—you can draw on me for money—write me and say how much money you will need in June and I will send the amount on the first of that month—give my love to all the folks . . ."

Edison was far from wealthy when he wrote that letter. But his intelligent labor was beginning to reward him. In time General Lefferts summoned Edison for a conference. Tom realized that the General was eager to acquire total control of his Universal Stock Ticker—an excellent invention, whose principles are used to this day—and other patents along this line on which Edison had been working.

As the inventor later told the story:

He called me into his office and said: "Now, young man, I want to close up the matter of your inventions. How much do you think you should receive?"

I had made up my mind that, taking into consideration the time and killing pace I was working at, I should be entitled to $5,000, but could get along with $3,000. When the psychological moment arrived, I hadn't the nerve to name such a large sum, so I said:

"Well, General, suppose you make me an offer."

Then he said: "How would $40,000 strike you?"

This caused me to come as near fainting as I

ever got. I was afraid he would hear my heart beat. I managed to say that I thought it was fair.

"All right, I will have a contract drawn; come around in three days and sign it, and I will give you the money."

As you may well imagine, Edison was on hand three days later. He signed the contract "without reading it" and was handed the first check he had ever received in his life (having previously been paid in cash for his services). The slip of paper with the large figures on it seemed utterly unreal, and completely unlike the enormous sum of $40,000, which it was supposed to represent.

Feeling lightheaded, Tom went to the bank and passed his precious paper through a barred window. The teller handed it back for endorsement—a formality new to Tom. Because of his deafness, Edison could not understand what the teller was saying. Obviously this check was worthless and the whole deal had been a fraud. In misery and desperation he went outdoors "to the large steps to let the cold sweat evaporate."

The General laughed when Edison told him the story, and sent him back with an employee who could

identify the young inventor. But the teller continued
the joke by handing Tom the $40,000 in small bills.
Edison crammed every pocket of his suit and overcoat with the bulging packets until he looked like the
fat man at a circus. He lay awake all night guarding
his treasure.

Next day the General thought the joke had gone
far enough. He helped Tom open his first bank account. Overnight the wandering telegrapher had become a man of property whose prospects were almost
unimaginable. Now he could operate his own factory
and laboratory and spend his busy hours at the profession he loved most of all—inventing useful objects
for humanity.

For the next six years Edison centered most of his ac-
tivity in the city of Newark, New Jersey, where he
could rent space for his factory and hire skilled workmen capable of learning complicated new processes.

In an old building at 10 and 12 Ward Street, he set
up his new business of manufacturing hundreds of
stock and gold tickers. For a time he was his own
foreman, supervising both the day and the night shift.
His typical working day was twenty hours, leaving

less than four for sleep. He ate irregularly, paid not the slightest attention to his health, smoked too many cigars, drank too much coffee, and seemed to thrive on this schedule.

Edison was a shrewd employer who quickly sensed the value of any worker. John Ott, an excellent mechanic, applied for a job. John was twenty, Tom Edison was twenty-two. The young men looked each other over, and in a few seconds realized they could work together.

"What do you want me to do?" Ott asked.

"Can you make one of these?" Edison inquired, pointing to a stock ticker.

"If I can't, you don't need to pay me," John said.

Ott produced one of the best examples of this model Edison had ever seen. He was soon Edison's first assistant, a dependable manager of production, willing to labor long and faithfully, and capable of directing scores of other mechanics.

Ott remembered that in those days Edison dressed carelessly. But he had a way of making work interesting. He had the rarest of all gifts, the ability to inspire his fellow workers. When a technician showed intelligence, zest, or endurance, this superior workman was well paid for his talents. Most of the men were on piecework, rewarded strictly in accordance with their ability to produce. This opportunity to earn in relation to one's skill attracted some of the best craftsmen on the Eastern seaboard.

Several foreign-born mechanics who applied for jobs with Edison lived to become celebrities in the field of electricity. Working side by side at the Ward Street factory were: Sigmund Bergmann, a German Jew who at first knew scarcely a word of English, and Sigmund Schuckert, also from Germany. Both eventually became multimillionaire manufacturers of electrical equipment. At the same bench labored another greatly talented mechanic, John Kruesi, a Swiss by birth. He would later follow Edison to Menlo Park and in time would become the engineer in charge of the Edison General Electric plant at Schenectady, New York.

An equally gifted employee was Charles Batchelor, long associated with Edison in later ventures. Batchelor was a handsome, dignified, bearded Englishman with hands delicately attuned to precise scientific work. Having come to America to install the machinery at the Clark Sewing Thread mills in Newark, he chose our country as a permanent home. Batchelor sensed in Edison a man of genius. Tom in his mid-twenties was still slender and youthful in appearance. He was clean-shaven (when he found time to shave). Around him were men much older than he, many of them sporting the luxuriant full beards of the era.

Nevertheless, Edison was known to all as the "Old Man"—the boss, the head of the tribe. He looked a little like Napoleon at the same age, and he sometimes used up his men almost as ruthlessly—on one occasion keeping the entire working force at the factory for sixty continuous hours until the "bugs" were worked out of a new ticker. But like all great commanders, he preferred to lead his men rather than to drive them. No employee could work as hard or as many hours as the "Old Man" himself.

While this tousle-haired, keen-eyed young manufacturer showed continuous talent in his simultaneous work on some forty inventions and in the technical management of his factories, his knowledge of finances left much to be desired. He kept no books except those in connection with the payroll. He had no cashbook or journal or ledger, merely two hooks, one for the bills he owed, and one for sums due him. The $40,000 he had received from Marshall Lefferts had long since disappeared. He now lived from hand to mouth, scraping together the money for the weekly payroll as best he could. Obviously he needed a bookkeeper, and eventually he hired one.

While still financially insecure, he wrote another affectionate letter to his father and mother in Port Huron, asking the perpetual questions: "Why don't you write to me and tell me the news? . . . How is mother getting along? . . . I am in a position now to let you have some cash, so you can write and say how much."

Edison's bank account could ill afford his present offer to buy for his mother and father a piece of property they coveted. His notes were being protested because they were often overdue. Sometimes the sheriff with his red flag could be kept from the door only by a daily payment of $5. But if his father and mother were in need, that claim came first.

I may be home sometime this winter—can't say when exactly, for I have a large amount of business to attend to . . . Give my love to all.

Your son,
THOMAS A.

Tom did not get home as he had hoped. His mother died on April 9, 1871, a few months after the letter was written. She lived only long enough to be proud of his earliest successes. Soon Tom was writing to offer his vital and independent old father a home and an easy job in Newark.

According to family tradition, the young inventor met Mary Stilwell at the entrance of his factory on a day of pouring rain. Mary and her sister Alice had taken shelter in the arched doorway. They seemed little more than schoolgirls, but Tom Edison, who had a shy admiration for the "condensed sunshine" of lovely womanhood, took a swift liking to pretty, modest Mary, who taught Sunday school at a Newark church. Often on Sunday he would have a horse and buggy at the church door waiting to take her for a drive through the New Jersey hills.

When Edison proposed, Mary's father protested that his daughter was much too young, and that the marriage would have to be postponed a year. To keep Mary near him, Tom gave her a job in the factory preparing one of his latest products, the newly invented paraffined paper. Although her eyes might be on her task, Miss Stilwell was not unaware of her employer, who from time to time found it necessary to supervise her work.

"Oh, Mr. Edison," she said to him one day, "I can always tell when you are near me."

During these years Edison was operating one, then two, and finally five factories in Newark. His busy brain was hard at work, principally on improvements of the telegraph. His three greatest inventions in that field were the automatic telegraph, the quadruplex telegraph, and the motograph.

The automatic telegraph, by simplest definition, is one which "needs no operator at the receiving end." Whether the moving tape receives the message with perforations, chemical stains, or printed letters, the principle is much the same. Electrical impulses carry the message, which is automatically recorded in a distant city.

Hand-operated telegraph keys can seldom send or receive more than fifty words a minute. Edison, after many laborious experiments, invented several methods of sending more than 1,000 words a minute. This was carefully verified by Lord Kelvin, one of the greatest scientists of his century.

Jay Gould might be called the "villain" of this story. He itched to get his hands on the Edison automatic telegraph inventions, not because he wished to improve the country's telegraphic service—his motives were seldom that high-minded—but because it would furnish him one more weapon in his carefully planned campaign to undermine the Western Union Telegraph Company.

Edison's automatic was controlled by a group of associates and backers. Gould "bought them out" with a promise of $4,000,000 worth of stock; then, having gained his objective, refused to pay any but a few individuals involved, although he did take over Edison's inventions and improvements. Court litigation went on for a third of a century. It was finally ruled that Gould had indeed virtually stolen the automatic telegraph. But the damages allowed were one dollar. So Edison was deprived of any reward for nearly three years of hard work.

It is surprising that Edison survived the six or seven years he spent on telegraphic inventions. It is probable that the only reason he did survive was because all the parties involved needed his help.

For instance, Edison's brilliant motograph principle, which twice earned him large rewards, was a direct outgrowth of this same struggle. One day William Orton, President of Western Union, asked Edison to come to his office. Orton was greatly disturbed. Jay Gould had acquired a basic patent of such importance to the Morse magnetic telegraph that Orton believed he could deprive Western Union of the use of the telegraph sounder and its retractile spring. What was needed was an entirely new approach to telegraphy—a new principle, and a new system. Tom Edison, with typical self-assurance, promised he would invent such a system, starting that very night.

Not only that night, and the next, but around the clock for many weeks Edison labored, making more than 2,000 experiments based on one of his recent discoveries. He had noticed in experimenting with an electric pencil, or stylus, on a moving tape that when an electrical impulse was sent through the stylus the tape moved more swiftly. Evidently the current made the tape slippery. Using this fundamental observation as a starting point, Edison finally came up with a completely workable new telegraph system. To use his own words: "I substituted a piece of chalk rotated

by a small electric motor for the magnet, and connected a sounder to a metallic finger resting on the
chalk."

Had Gould enforced his claim to a monopoly on
the retractile spring in Morse's magnetic telegraph,
Western Union might today be using the motograph.
But Gould, realizing that his card had been trumped,
dropped the matter. Western Union continued to use
the old Morse magnetic system, putting Edison's startling new invention in the safe.

In this case, however, Edison did receive $100,000
for his work—a sum which he requested be paid to
him in equal yearly installments over a period of seventeen years. He knew only too well that were it
given him in a lump sum, he would squander it immediately on new laboratory equipment.

Worrying about his old father, fighting to meet the
payrolls of five factories and grappling at times with
more than 100 inventions, Edison wondered in the
few quiet moments he ever allowed himself whether
he would be able to keep afloat in the stormy seas of
telegraphy.

Meanwhile, still another of Edison's complex inventions was inspired by the continuing drama
within the telegraph industry. Ever since his years as

a wandering telegrapher, Tom had been working on the problem of sending two messages over one wire simultaneously. Eventually he patented the "duplex," a method for sending two messages at the same time over a single wire.

One day Orton of Western Union asked Tom why four simultaneous messages could not be flashed over one wire, two in each direction! No reason at all, Edison said. He would tackle the problem immediately. Orton pointed out that it would save the telegraph company millions of dollars, since it would again double the capacity of their entire system. Tom realized that his own reward should be substantial.

Using eight operators, four at each end, Edison labored night after night in the cavernous basement of Western Union in New York City. His wires were strung from room to room as though between cities. Moving from one end of the telegraph to the other Tom varied the currents, tinkered with the apparatus, and racked his brain for the elusive answer. He himself admitted that this particular problem was almost beyond his mental powers.

When at last he thought he had found a solution, he set up a "quadruplex" connection between New York City and Albany, inviting William Orton (and other Western Union officials) to witness the results. Wind, rain, thunder, and lightning intervened. The telegraphic reception was so poor that Orton was far from impressed. He handed Edison a check for $5,000 "on account"—pin money to the desperate inventor, who was in danger of losing his home as well as his factories. At this point Orton left for Europe.

General Eckert, long a Western Union executive, told Edison that he would probably never receive another cent from Orton. Eckert added, however, that he knew a man who might be willing to buy "Edison's rights" in the quadruplex. Edison said he didn't know what his private share of the rights might be but that he knew they were far in excess of the $5,000.

Next day the interested party turned out to be none other than Jay Gould, who had been awaiting just such an opportunity. Edison again explained all the complications, but Gould was pleased to pay him $30,000 for whatever rights the inventor still possessed. This time Gould actually kept his promise and paid the money.

Edison worked only briefly for Gould, then returned to his former close association with Western Union. And William Orton was only too happy to welcome him back.

For the time being, Edison was able to save his Newark factories. But he was growing weary of the unceasing headaches of Newark, and the crafty dealings of the telegraphic industry. Tom wished to turn from manufacturing to invention, and from telegraphy to greener fields of exploration. He needed peace, quiet, and time in which to think. He longed for the solitude of the country.

On Christmas Day, 1871, Thomas Alva Edison married his attractive fellow worker, Mary Stilwell. They say that he almost forgot to come home from the factory in time for his wedding. It is told that at first he refused to wear white gloves over his acid-stained, honest hands. Whatever the truth of this folklore, the marriage was a happy one which, in a few years, produced three children—a bright and pretty daughter named Marion, a son named Thomas Alva, and later a third child named William.

What his little family needed, reasoned the inventor, was a good home on a hill amid trees and grass and flowers. And that was exactly what they were about to find in the village of Menlo Park in a pleasant rural area of New Jersey.

5

THE TELEPHONE AND THE PHONOGRAPH

"In trying to perfect a thing, I sometimes run straight up against a granite wall a hundred feet high."

Thomas A. Edison

Edison was now entering upon the most productive period of his long and fertile life. He was not yet thirty when in 1876 he moved the base of his operations to Menlo Park. Within the next few years he was to invent, among many other devices, the carbon telephone transmitter, the phonograph, and the first practical incandescent electric light.

Edison told a friend at this time that he hoped to produce one new invention every ten days. Over a period of several decades he managed to approach that record, bringing to the United States Patent Office, on the average, about two inventions a month. His contributions to human progress, during his most creative years, challenge the record of any inventor of recorded history.

Often it is asked why Edison chose Menlo Park, a tiny village of only seven or eight houses, with little to offer except fresh air, solitude, and a view. In part the choice may have been a happy accident. According to one version of the story, when old Sam Edison was invited to Newark, Tom gave him a pleasant assignment. He furnished his father a horse and buggy and asked him to scout the nearby regions of New Jersey for a likely spot for the new laboratory.

By good luck or good judgment, Sam chose a hilltop midway between New York and Philadelphia on the Old Post Road. Here there was an inn, a grocery store, and a little station on the Pennsylvania Railroad. Best of all, perhaps, was the panorama of woods and farmers' fields as seen from this windy prominence— a view almost as beautiful in its way as that which once delighted the picknickers who climbed Sam Edison's observation tower in Port Huron.

Tom himself examined several possible locations on succeeding Sundays late in 1875, then agreed with his father on the virtues of Menlo Park. Quite possibly Mary Stilwell Edison had something to do with the choice. On a large corner lot facing the Post Road stood a three-story white clapboard house which would comfortably shelter the Edison family. Here, but a short distance from the laboratory, the Edison children could safely play on the gently sloping lawn. Mary knew that spring would blanket these hills with violets and anemones.

Samuel Edison was a good carpenter and contractor. Following plans drawn by his son, he supervised the construction of the laboratory, while Mary and her children moved into the big house. Mary's sister Alice, whom Edison had met on the same rainy day he met Mary, also made her home with the Edisons. The household employed five servants: Maria, Minnie, Susan, Delia, and Mose. The last-named was the groom who tended the horses in the big stable behind the house.

At right angles to the Post Road ran the only important street in Menlo Park. This short thoroughfare, named Christie Street, had a boardwalk for a distance of some 850 feet between the Edison home and laboratory. By day or night for the next several years Edison was to be seen traversing this walk. "He generally wore a skull cap or a farmer's wide-rimmed straw, carried both hands in the front pockets of his trousers according to the style of the time, and strolled along with head bent in thought."

The laboratory was situated on a knoll, ". . . looking for all the world like a country meeting-house minus the steeple . . . a long, two-story, white frame building . . . surrounded by a white picket fence." This was Tom Edison's shop as seen by a writer of the time. One stepped into the first floor from a front porch to find ". . . a little front office, from which a small library is partitioned off. Next . . . a large room with glass cases filled with models of his inventions."

The entire second floor was the laboratory itself, lighted by many-paned windows. The walls were lined with shelves containing thousands of bottles of chemicals. "Scattered through the room are tables covered with electrical instruments . . . microscopes, spectroscopes, etc. In the center . . . a rack full of galvanic batteries . . . In the rear . . . a fine pipe organ . . . At the opposite end of the room stands Mr. Edison, [expressing the opinion that] there is no philosopher like Herbert Spencer, no writer like Victor Hugo, and no poet like Edgar A. Poe."

To this laboratory Edison brought several of his most gifted helpers. "Honest" John Kruesi ran the machine shop. Deft-fingered, swift-minded Charles Batchelor and the always dependable John Ott were among his most talented assistants. These and the other employees were "the boys." Edison, more than ever, was the "Old Man." Despite his youth and his democratic ways, he was the guiding genius.

"Everything always worked in that old laboratory," Edison was to say in later years. But, in truth, he sometimes ran up against that "granite wall a hundred feet high." This was particularly true when he tackled the problem of the telephone transmitter.

Three talented men were striving individually at this moment to work a major miracle—the swift transference of various sounds, including the human voice, by wire. One was Alexander Graham Bell (1847–1922), a Boston teacher of elocution, schooled in Edinburgh and London. A second was Elisha Gray (1835–1901), a Quaker carpenter and electrician from Ohio, trained at Oberlin College. The third was Thomas Alva Edison (1847–1931).

All three were working on systems to send many messages simultaneously over a single telegraph wire. All had hit upon the possibility of using tuning forks of various pitches to send these multiple messages, keyed to like tuning forks at the other end. The logical conclusion derived from the "harmonic telegraph" was that the human voice itself could be sent by wire.

Few inventions come into this world full-blossomed from a single brain. Most are the product of many minds and many thoughtful years. In the instance of the telephone, the scientific principle was defined, perhaps for the first time, by a Frenchman named Charles Bourseul, a soldier in Algeria.

Wrote Bourseul in 1854: "We know that sounds are made by vibrations, and are made sensible to the ear by the same vibrations . . . Suppose a man speaks near a movable disk . . . that this disk alternately makes and breaks the connection with the battery; you may have at a distance another disk which will simultaneously execute the same vibrations."

Bourseul rightly reasoned that one might thus send the human voice by electrical impulse over miles of wire. However, he did not try to demonstrate the truth of his theory through experimentation, and apparently never even attempted to invent a "telephone."

A German professor named Philipp Reis, however, did make the attempt. His crude device, which could not be kept "in tune" for more than a few seconds at a time, came to the attention of Edison's friend William Orton, President of Western Union, who suggested that Edison try to improve it to the point of workability.

Meanwhile Alexander Graham Bell and Elisha Gray, unknown to each other, were progressing rapidly with their "speaking telegraphs," or telephones. Bell filed a patent for the telephone only a few hours before Gray, who for the rest of his life was embittered by this sad turn of fate.

The Bell telephone was demonstrated at the Philadelphia Centennial in 1876 to fascinated thousands. Edison always gave Bell credit for producing the first practical telephone—particularly in respect to reception. But it was Edison himself who invented the carbon transmitter which made the modern telephone a reality. For years telephones carried the names of both Bell and Edison on every instrument.

Bell's instrument had only one diaphragm, which was held to the mouth when speaking, and to the ear when listening. This magnetically controlled device was useful for reproducing sound, but it failed to capture many fine gradations of voice when used as a transmitter. To correct this difficulty, Edison suggested a separate mouthpiece, a continuous contact between the diaphragm and the wires, and, finally, amplification of the current.

To effect this magic, Edison conducted thousands of experiments. Between the disk and the wire he

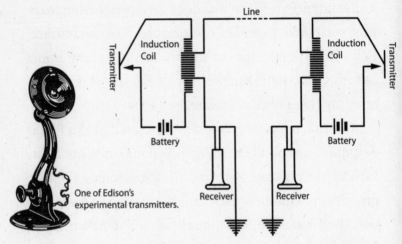

Edison's Telephone

Line

Induction Coil — Transmitter — Battery — Receiver

Induction Coil — Transmitter — Battery — Receiver

One of Edison's experimental transmitters.

Diagram showing how Edison changed the telephone by adding the transmitter and introducing a primary circuit from an induction coil.

tried fluids such as water and mercury, fibers such as silk, and silk disks impregnated with carbon. None was totally successful.

Perhaps at this point he may have remembered something he had learned from Parker's *School Compendium*: the ability of solid, elastic bodies to communicate sound. Obviously what Edison needed in his telephone transmitter was a solid but elastic body, fastened firmly to both the diaphragm and the wires.

After filling scores of laboratory notebooks with

experiments, he hit upon carbon buttons molded from lampblack. These miraculously sensitive little buttons proved capable (through compression or expansion) of translating vibrations of the human voice directly into the electrical resistances in the carbon. Thus the most subtle variations of electrical current, when amplified, could be sent any distance —ultimately around the world.

Alf Swanson, the lusty night watchman, who sported a magnificent mustache, was given the smoky job of tending a whole battery of kerosene lamps in the little "lamp shed" to the west of the laboratory. These lamps were turned very high to produce as much soot as possible on the inside of the glass chimneys. Each night, Alf, on his rounds, entered this shed to scrape the lamp chimneys and mold the carbon into buttons, which he carefully weighed and packed, for use in carbon telephone transmitters. One day a reporter visiting Menlo Park came rushing in to tell Edison that the lamps in the lamp shed were in terrible shape, all turned much too high and smoking their chimneys jet-black. The joke was on the embarrassed reporter.

Edison sold his patent for the carbon telephone transmitter to Western Union for $100,000—

payment again to be spread over seventeen years. Western Union, after the clash with the Bell interests, finally sold out to Bell, collecting, however, a stiff royalty for use of the transmitter. Later, from English financiers, Edison received 30,000 pounds (about $150,000) for a loud-speaking telephone receiver.

It was never all work and no play with Edison. He loved to romp with Dot and Dash, as he called his daughter Marion and his first son, Thomas Alva. He would come to their parties from the laboratory, still in his working clothes, would stand on his head for their amusement or make shadow pictures behind a lighted screen. Once he erected a fifteen-foot pole which the children were asked to climb to obtain the coins at the top. When little Thomas Alva proved a poor climber, his father rubbed a little resin on the knees of his trousers and the boy could climb as well as his tomboy sister.

In summer the inventor occasionally took his family to Boynton Beach, where he taught the children to swim. In winter there were sleigh rides with now and again a well-planned upset in soft drifts of deep snow. Marion in particular loved all these excursions.

A toy which Edison fashioned for his children helped him to invent the magical device we call the phonograph. The plaything was a little man attached to a telephone diaphragm. The vibrations of the human voice made this toy figure appear to saw wood. This set Edison to thinking. If the human voice could create such motion, why couldn't the motion be re-translated into the human voice?

Edison was already aware that he could capture, on a revolving disk or a cylinder, the dots and dashes of the telegraph. Through varying indentations in a spiral groove these sounds could be accurately reproduced at any time. One day when his mechanism ran wild and raced in ever faster revolutions, Edison heard sounds which were much like the human voice. Now he was certain that he was on the track of a great new invention.

Hastily he sketched the design for an odd little contraption. It had a crank, a grooved cylinder, a floating arm, supporting a needle at one end and attached to a telephone diaphragm at the other. He gave this sketch to John Kruesi, boss of his machine shop, and told him to make it. John had not the slightest idea what the machine was supposed to do. But he had an uncanny ability to construct any device Edison suggested.

When the mysterious little machine had been carefully constructed, Kruesi brought it to Edison's desk. Associates gathered around, as mystified as Honest John, and as curious.

"What is this for?" he asked.

"This machine must talk," said Edison.

Bets were made against any such weird possibility: $1, $2, free cigars against a barrel of apples! Edison happily took all these bets. He asked for a sheet of tinfoil, which he attached to the cylinder. Then he began to turn the crank. The tinfoil tore, and some of the laboratory men pointed significantly at their foreheads and thought of the free cigars. But Charles Batchelor knew his chief.

"Keep your shirt on," he told the other men.

Undaunted by the skeptical smiles, Edison asked for another sheet of tinfoil. This time he glued it carefully to the cylinder. Then into the little mouthpiece, as he turned the crank, he recited the well-known nursery rhyme:

> *"Mary had a little lamb,*
> *Its fleece was white as snow,*

And everywhere that Mary went
The lamb was sure to go."

Putting the needle back at the starting point, he again turned the crank, and from the diaphragm of this amazing new machine came the ghostly sound of his own voice:

"Mary had a little lamb,
Its fleece was white as snow —"

"Gott im Himmel!" cried the frightened Kruesi, who all unknowing had constructed this diabolical and heavenly machine.

Edison himself was startled and amazed. Most inventions of a major nature took him years to perfect. But here was an utterly new device which worked on the very first test. In a flash of inspiration he had created the phonograph, an invention which in years to come would record the greatest singers of the age for generations yet unborn; a machine that could talk, laugh, sneeze, cough, and play symphonies. Here in one unforgettable moment had been born a form of immortality—a permanent record of the human voice. No wonder they were beginning to call young Tom Edison the "Wizard of Menlo Park."

6

THE ELECTRIC LIGHT

"The incandescent light was the hardest one of all; it took many years not only of concentrated thought but also of world-wide research."

Thomas A. Edison

One reason why Edison had moved to the breezy hilltop called Menlo Park was the hope that he might enjoy a certain amount of privacy. Occasionally on a pleasant day in spring he imagined himself "Plato on a butterfly"—a philosopher with wings. He liked to gaze off across the valleys blossoming with fruit trees, or roll in the dandelions with Dot and Dash.

With the invention of the phonograph, however, his privacy was suddenly invaded. Crowds came to Menlo Park to see the miraculous machine which could talk. Demonstrations in New York and even at the White House in Washington, D.C., exhausted the young inventor as no amount of hard work could tire him. Obviously he needed a rest, and so he took the first vacation he had permitted himself in ten years.

Edison combined his vacation with yet another scientific experiment. Recently he had invented a supersensitive device for registering variations of temperature down to the millionth part of a degree Fahrenheit. He called this new invention the "tasimeter."

Everyone in the world knows something about Edison's phonograph, telephone transmitter, incandescent light, and moving-picture camera, but not one in a million could tell you about the tasimeter. Here again as in the telephone, Edison used a carbon button, varying the pressure to increase or decrease the resistance to an electric current.

The human hand, held thirty feet from the tasimeter, was warm enough to affect the reading on the dial. So was "a maiden's blush." It was even possible to detect the heat coming from such a distant star as Arcturus. Now Edison hoped to test, during a complete eclipse of the sun, the temperature of the fringe of light or "corona" which one sees during a total eclipse.

The path of the eclipse was far to the west. Physicists and astronomers from all over the world were gathering at the village of Rawlins, Wyoming

Territory, in midsummer, 1878, to be on hand for the eclipse which would occur on July 29. Edison and his tasimeter were aboard one of the special railroad cars taking the scientists west.

In those days the West was still wild. Great herds of shaggy buffalo roamed everywhere over the unbroken prairies. It was but two summers since Custer and his 264 men had been slaughtered by the Sioux at the Little Big Horn. Edison himself went hunting in Ute country where only a month later a major and his thirty men were ambushed and slaughtered. All this, to a person of Edison's adventuresome temperament, was a welcome variation from the safe and civilized regions of the East.

Rawlins proved to be a shabby little frontier town with a tiny hotel soon filled to bursting. Edison's roommate was Marshall Fox, a star reporter for the New York *Herald*. They struck up a friendship which lasted for many years.

Edison's "observatory," where he set up his telescope and tasimeter, was an old chicken house. This wooden structure, which rocked wildly in the wind, was no help to a scientist trying for delicate measurements. Nor were the hens very accommodating. When the eclipse occurred they thought it was nightfall, and therefore came clucking and crowding into the henhouse. To top Edison's misfortunes, the heat of the corona of the sun was about ten times too great to be measured on the sensitive dial. But Edison did have the satisfaction of watching the needle turn swiftly when, at the last possible moment, he was able to focus his instruments.

Edison's western trip, which lasted for nearly two months, was in every other way a success. He was allowed to ride for many miles on the cowcatcher of a locomotive. With Marshall Fox he stalked a stuffed jack rabbit while the practical jokers nearly collapsed with laughter, and on another occasion he was petrified when a stuffed bear "leaped" at him from beside the trail. He visited San Francisco, Virginia City, and Yosemite, hiked scores of miles, and filled his lungs with good mountain air. Edison, who according to his father "never had a boyhood," was having a taste of boyhood now.

Returning to Menlo Park, refreshed by nature and the playful antics of his friends in the Far West, Edison was eager to get back to work. He began to think seriously of his next great experiment—the attempt to produce an inexpensive, safe, and practical form of electric light. As his notebooks show, he felt certain that he could replace illuminating gas with a better method for lighting homes and offices. He knew that many other men had tried and failed, but this seldom daunted Edison.

Actually, experiments along this line had been progressing slowly for nearly seventy-five years. Sir Humphry Davy's arc lamp was based on an entirely different principle. However, even in the realm of incandescence, Edison was by no means the first to visualize the electric lamp. At least thirty other inventors had worked on the problem before him. For various reasons none of his predecessors had produced a really practical electric light, although at least one, J. W. Swan, was approaching that point.

Arc lights were used in the street lighting of many cities long before Edison began his experiments. But these lights, consisting of two sticks of carbon brought near enough together to permit a brilliant electric arc, hissed, sputtered, dropped intensely hot sparks and frequently went out of commission. Obviously they were not safe or sensible for indoor lighting.

Edison rightly analyzed the troubles with all previous incandescent lights enclosed in glass globes. First, they used thick, low-resistance units of metal or carbon which necessitated a fantastic amount of electric current. Second, the incandescent substance in the globe swiftly burned out. Third, no method had yet been found to "subdivide electricity" the way gas could be rationed to every jet. Fourth, electric generators had never surpassed fifty per cent efficiency. Edison believed they must be ninety per cent efficient to make electrical systems possible.

Any one of these four problems left unsolved was in itself fatal to the future of electric lighting. Taken together they made its future seem preposterous. With boundless courage, Edison proposed to solve all four problems.

Accompanied by Professor Barker of the University of Pennsylvania and Professor Chandler of Columbia, Edison now made a trip to Ansonia, Connecticut, to see the electric lights of William Wallace, an inventor and brass manufacturer. The occasion was a pleasant one, but Edison soon found that Wallace had not discovered the solution to any of the four major problems. Back home in Menlo Park, he rolled up his sleeves and went to work.

He was sure that he was on the right track—and

that Wallace was not. Barely a week after his trip to Ansonia, Edison granted an interview to a New York *Sun* reporter, insisting very prematurely that he had discovered the way to substitute electricity for illuminating gas ". . . through an entirely different process . . . When it is known how I have accomplished my object, everyone will wonder why they have never thought of it." Instead of ten lights from an "electric machine" Edison promised "a thousand . . . ten thousand . . . Indeed the number may be said to be infinite." In a burst of prophetic optimism he predicted that the wire "that brings light to you will also bring power and heat. With the power you can run an elevator, a sewing machine or any other mechanical contrivance."

It has been suggested that Edison knowingly made such announcements for the purpose of putting himself and his staff on the mettle. Having promised a miracle, it was then only necessary to produce one. But on this occasion he seriously misjudged his timing, for he had many granite walls to climb before he could make good his boast.

There were several swift reactions to the story, not all of them pleasant. The world at large was thrilled by such a promise. But the illuminating gas industry went into a near-panic. Gas stocks fell sharply in London and New York. If the inspired inventor of the telephone transmitter and the phonograph said he could make electric light, power, and heat cheaply available, what would happen to the $1,500,000,000 now invested in gas companies?

Previous inventors of clumsy and inefficient electric lights immediately began screaming that Edison was "stealing" their idea. Theoretical scientists, certain that "division of electricity" was impossible, called Edison's claim of its solution pure fraud, a will-o'-the-wisp, and a false hope. The young inventor smiled grimly and only worked the harder.

How would it have seemed to be a bright boy helping Edison during that magical year in which he invented the incandescent light? Fortunately there was such a boy, and he has left us a wonderfully detailed record.

His name was Francis Jehl (pronounced *Yale*), and he had been a junior clerk in the law office of Grosvenor P. Lowrey, a Wall Street friend and financial backer of Thomas Edison. Francis was so deeply interested in science that after his day's work in the office he spent long hours attending night classes at the

Cooper Union school studying chemistry, "natural philosophy," and higher algebra. When his employer told him that there was a chance that he might join Mr. Edison's staff at Menlo Park, Francis accepted the possibility "with much eagerness."

He arrived at the laboratory on a raw and dreary day which in no way dampened his youthful excitement. Climbing the wooden steps from the railway station, he made his way up Christie Street, and through the gate to the yard surrounding the laboratory, satchel in hand.

"Chained to a hickory tree near the east side of the laboratory was what seemed to be an unusually large dog, apparently asleep. I stepped aside to bestow a friendly pat upon its head, but as I came nearer suddenly the head turned and you can imagine my astonishment to find the creature was not a dog, but a shaggy bear."

Francis did not stop for another look. He made a "bee-line for the front veranda," dashed into the laboratory, and quickly closed the door behind him. Only later did he learn that the bear was a fairly harmless pet.

Francis introduced himself to Johnny Randolph,

the office boy, who told the new arrival to go upstairs and "hang around" until Mr. Edison noticed him. Young Jehl climbed the stairs, his heart thumping. There before him was the laboratory he had dreamed about, with its rows of bottles, its instrument tables, and the impressive pipe organ at the north end. There too was Thomas Edison himself, "deeply engrossed in a platinum lamp" on which he was experimenting. Edison was so busy that at first he didn't notice Francis, who waited shyly. Meanwhile the boy's eyes roamed hungrily around the laboratory, at last discovering the "wonderful phonograph . . . the marvel of the world." This young man was to outlive Edison and all the other helpers at Menlo Park. But even in his seventies Jehl would remember how he felt at that moment, as he watched the already famous inventor: "To the eighteen-year-old youth waiting, hat in hand, for an interview, he was the greatest figure among living men."

At length Edison looked up with an expression of friendly interest. "Hello! What do you want?" Francis stammered his answer, then to cover his confusion, produced the letter of introduction from Mr. Lowrey.

"Oh, yes, Mr. Lowrey spoke to me about you. What experience have you had?"

Now the boy found his tongue. Swiftly he told Edison of his love for science, his night classes at Cooper Union and how he had operated the "intercommunicating telegraph" in Lowrey's office.

"When can you start?"

"Right away."

"Well, I need the cells of my Bunsen battery cleaned and filled . . . I'll show you how to do it."

Francis already knew how to clean and fill the many cells of the battery, for he had been assigned that long and tedious job at Cooper Union. He now began the many hours of work involved. When he was finished Edison inspected the result.

"I see you know the ropes," he said.

Cleaning and refilling the battery cells had taken the whole afternoon, and dusk had settled. Edison remarked that his new assistant might "take the rest of the day" and directed him to "Aunt Sally" Jordan's boardinghouse, which would soon become famous as the first residence in America to be lighted with incandescent electric lamps. Francis Jehl went down the dark, windy street carrying his satchel, his heart singing. The hours would be long, the pay would be poor, but he was now the young helper of the Wizard of Menlo Park. He was, in fact, the Sorcerer's Apprentice.

New assistants, new buildings, new financing—all three were needed if Edison were to have the best opportunity to create the new electric light.

Another staff member who made his appearance at Mrs. Jordan's boardinghouse at about this time was the brilliant young mathematician Francis Upton, who had been trained at Princeton and in Germany. He had the cultural polish which Edison lacked, and he had the training in mathematics which was needed to supplement Edison's common sense and keen intuition. During the coming months he would solve many brain-paralyzing equations in helping Edison make revolutionary improvements in the electric generator, and in charting the hitherto unexplored realm of the "subdivision of electricity."

Months later a third new employee came briefly to Mrs. Jordan's boardinghouse, before moving into the little frame shack behind the laboratory. He was Ludwig Boehm, the German-trained glass blower, who wore a jaunty little fraternity cap from his

German school and played sentimental songs on the zither while yodeling his accompaniment. He had been hired by "Meester Ettison" to blow "ze boolbs." The inventor treated him with the consideration due his real talent. But Edison once admitted that Ludwig was the "most conceited man" he had ever met. Some of the boys imitated the glass blower's yodeling, which always made Boehm furious. And yet it was this same conceited little man who blew fanciful, almost fairy-like figures from glass for Edison's children, and sometimes charmed even the savage breasts of his fellow workers with his music.

Other salty characters at Menlo Park were "Daddy" Edison (as the workers affectionately called the inventor's father) and J. U. Mackenzie, the stationmaster who had taught Edison telegraphy. These two storytelling cronies were considered "guests." They wandered around the laboratory at will, worked if they felt inclined, played with the Edison children, and vied for the comfortable red leather sofa, the perfect spot to take afternoon naps.

The beautiful sofa was but one of the many handsome pieces of furniture in the new library and office building, constructed just to the southeast of the laboratory—a two-story brick structure with gleaming wood paneling, shelves for many books, cherry-wood desks and tables, and large upholstered chairs. Best of all was that sofa on which Edison seldom had a chance to rest if Daddy Edison or J. U. Mackenzie could get there first.

One purpose of this expensive building, and of a second new brick building housing the workshop, was to impress the financial backers. Edison deplored such extravagance on mere buildings; but Grosvenor P. Lowrey, who came to Edison's financial rescue at this time, insisted upon them. Lowrey had assumed the difficult task of convincing several of his wealthy clients that Edison would indeed invent a practical, profitable electric light and that he deserved adequate backing. Among Lowrey's associates in the newly formed Edison Electric Light Company was an extremely right "silent partner," J. P. Morgan. Such tycoons, in their frock coats and high silk hats, needed to be impressed by the solidity of the new venture before putting up the $300,000 capital needed. So Lowrey suggested the new buildings, which rose through another form of magic—the magic of cold cash.

Nevertheless, it was the old clapboard laboratory which radiated the real enchantment in that group of buildings. Seeing its windows shining at night with the harsh glare of the burning gas jets, glimpsing the shadowy figures still at work over the mysterious tables of apparatus, hearing the rich tones of the organ accompanying the winter wind, young Francis Jehl could visualize this Wizard's lair as indeed a cave of wonders, awaiting only Aladdin's perfect lamp.

Another reason why Francis Jehl looked upon the laboratory as a scene from the *Arabian Nights* was the store of precious metals which were kept in locked cabinets at the northern end of the second floor of the laboratory, just behind the pipe organ. Here one might find zirconium, ruthenium, titanium, rhodium, barium, platinum, and many other rare and costly minerals, all being tested as possible "filaments" (the word Edison used) for the incandescent electric light.

Quite possibly Edison remembered from Parker's *School Compendium* a truth he had learned at the age of eleven. Wrote Parker, "Platina [that is, platinum] is the most ductile of all metals. It can be drawn into wire scarcely larger than a spider's web."

We have seen that Edison had correctly analyzed

one of the major errors in previous incandescent lamps: thick, low-resistant rods of glowing metal or carbon, necessitating dangerously powerful and ruinously uneconomical amounts of electric current. What was called for, of course, were cobweb-thin, high-resistant "filaments" which required only a moderate and inexpensive flow of the electrical "fluid."

Other experimenters had tried platinum in rods, and in thick wires. It remained for Edison to reduce the filament to a thread, and to place that thread in a bulb largely deprived of its normal content of air, thus reducing the rapidity of oxidation; for without oxygen, nothing can burn.

Three difficulties immediately arose. Platinum was too rare and too expensive for the purpose. Its melting point was not far above its point of incandescence. And, finally, no vacuum pump Edison possessed could eliminate enough of the air in a bulb to prevent oxidation. In short, these expensive platinum filaments, while they gave a brief, bright light, swiftly burned out.

Attacking these problems systematically in his usual logical manner, Edison started a world-wide search for platinum, hoping to increase its quantity and lower its cost. He devised ingenious means for automatically breaking the current when the platinum became overheated. Finally he developed better vacuum pumps to eliminate virtually the last trace of air in the bulbs.

Despite all this, his platinum lamps were a failure, and the $50,000 which had so far been advanced to him was gone—burned out like the many platinum filaments with which he had experimented. More money was needed, but the backers demanded a demonstration of progress before digging deeper into the pledged $300,000 of total capital.

Edison grimly complied. To prove his curiously dismal point he invited Grosvenor P. Lowrey, J. P. Morgan and the other financiers to come to Menlo Park on a blustering winter night late in 1878. These stockholders toiled their way up Christie Street to the wind-swept hilltop only to witness a planned fiasco.

The inventor had arranged his bulbs in racks along the wall of the laboratory. One bulb after another was lighted for a few splendid, gleaming moments, only to die an inglorious death, plunging the big room into darkness.

"There you go," said Edison, "you see the system is not practical." What was needed, he said, was more time, more experimentation, more money. The company could not hope to win with bulbs which lasted minutes at the most.

At a post-mortem held in the comfortable new library, Grosvenor P. Lowrey rose to the occasion. He persuaded the highly reluctant moneymen that his friend Thomas Edison would finally discover the solution, and that another sizable sum should be advanced. The inventor was to be given one more chance. But the atmosphere that evening was far from cheerful, and Edison knew that he now must win swiftly or go down in disgrace.

To add to his worries, Edison was having serious trouble with his eyes from long hours of gazing into glowing bulbs. His ears were also giving him intense pain until (to quote his sister-in-law, Alice) he sometimes wore the nap from the bedroom rug with his heels, silently enduring his agony. Newspapers and scientific journals were attacking him as a fraud. For once in his long, brave life he told a reporter that he often wondered why he continued with his day-and-night labors, only to be doubted and cheated of his just rewards. Even the greatest men have their moments of self-doubt; but their true greatness lies in their ability to rise above such moments.

It is permissible to lose a battle, but not a war. To men and nations of quality, a brief defeat can be a healthful tonic. Thomas A. Edison reacted in the manner of greatness. He now planned his campaign with the shrewdness of Napoleon and the determination of Grant. He had promised the world a practical incandescent light, and he would produce that miracle or ruin his health in the attempt.

Most human beings feel satisfied if they have worked for forty hours in any given week. Edison usually labored more than one hundred hours a week. Few were the members of his "insomnia squad" who could match his endurance, let alone his mental alertness.

Until April, 1879, the Menlo Park inventor continued to try platinum for a filament. Shortly thereafter he began toying with the idea of carbon—that black magic from which the white magic of the telephone transmitter and the tasimeter had emerged.

One day, while casually rolling a bit of lampblack between his fingers, he realized that he had produced a possible filament for an electric bulb. Bending this sticky black thread into a horseshoe, and baking it to surprising hardness in his laboratory furnace, he now began a new series of several thousand experiments. Slowly and patiently he labored, undaunted by failure after failure. Someday soon he would make good his promise to invent a successful bulb.

To achieve a carbon filament which would serve his purpose he tried every conceivable substance and fiber. He even baked the beard-hairs of J. U. Mackenzie, Charles Batchelor, and others (always there were bets as to whose beard would glow the longest in the electric bulb).

Paper, pasteboard, cotton thread, almost any vegetable fiber—no possible source of carbon was neglected. In each case the filament was carbonized with care. At least fifty per cent of the filaments were lost in the baking process. Another ten per cent were shattered while being placed in Boehm's glass bulbs. More casualties resulted when Francis Jehl began his delicate task, with the mercury pumps, of depleting the air. At the maximum, the entire laboratory force could produce but three experimental incandescent globes in a week of hard work. Then the "life-tests" would begin. Usually the bulbs gleamed for a few minutes or, at most, a few hours.

Thomas Edison was not the only laboratory

worker whose health suffered from this schedule of ceaseless labor. Small globules of mercury spilled on the floor from the pumps which Francis Jehl operated began to affect the teeth of all the workers. Even young men with healthy and gleaming ivories found their teeth shockingly and amazingly loose. One practical joker filled his mouth with large white beans, and came into the laboratory with a pained expression on his face. "I'm losing my teeth," he moaned, and began spurting the white beans from his mouth. They rattled realistically on the wooden floor.

Everyone, including Edison, rushed to view the tragedy, then roared with joyous relief. But Edison, who realized the seriousness of the situation, knew that something must be done. Through his excellent knowledge of chemistry, he devised a mouthwash to counteract the mercury poisoning. There was rarely a problem that Edison could not solve when he gave the matter thought.

Francis Jehl, although he had been with Edison for less than a year, had swiftly become an important and dependable assistant. Occasionally his name was mentioned in the newspaper stories about Menlo

Park. His most important duty, as we have seen, was to handle the complicated mercury pumps which removed the air from the experimental light bulbs. More than half a century later Jehl could still remember exactly what happened on the historic October days of 1879 when the first practical electric lamp was born.

After experimenting with metals so rare and costly they were almost unobtainable, Edison had discovered that carbonized cotton thread, which cost virtually nothing, was far better for a filament than platinum or any other precious metal he had tried.

On October 18 Edison carefully carbonized a loop of thread in the furnace, and Charles Batchelor, the only man with enough skill to handle the delicate filament placed it in the bulb. Now Francis began hours of labor (supervised by Edison), exhausting the air from the bulb. Finally Boehm was called to seal the bulb, which was now ready for its life test. The current was turned on and the thread began to glow. But let Francis tell the story:

> That Sunday night, long after the other men had gone, Edison and I kept a death-watch to note any convulsions or other last symptoms the lamp might give when expiring.

The lamp, however, did not expire! In the morning [after a not unusual day and night of continuous labor] we were relieved by Batchelor, Upton and Force. The lamp continued to burn brilliantly all that day, passing the 24-hour mark. We were stirred with hope as each hour passed . . . General good humor existed all around . . .

The night of the 20th of October again brought quiet to the laboratory as the watch continued, this time composed of Edison, Batchelor and me. During the night between the 20th and the 21st, Edison, judging from the appearance of the lamp still burning without a flaw, seemed satisfied that the first solid foundation of the future of electric lighting had now been laid.

The lamp held out heroically that night and the following day until, between one and two o'clock in the afternoon of Tuesday, October 21st, 1879, it had attained more than forty hours of life—the longest existence yet achieved by an incandescent lamp. The "boys" from all departments came to take a squint at the little wonder and to express their joy.

Edison now increased the current higher and higher, "until, in a dazzle of brightness, it gave out."

"If it will burn that number of hours," said Edison, "I know I can make it burn a hundred." Indeed he soon had a bulb, made from a slender carbonized horseshoe of pasteboard, which burned for 170 hours. Success was at hand.

Francis Jehl was as elated as Edison himself. The Sorcerer's Apprentice had served his master well. From Menlo Park would spread the great white magic which soon would illuminate the entire world. October 21 would ever after be celebrated as Edison Lamp Day.

Edison's Wall Street backers pleaded with him to be more cautious. The young inventor's inclination was to share his secrets with any stranger who visited the laboratory, rival inventors included. This threatened the financiers' investment in the Edison Electric Light Company. Since Edison had not yet patented his carbon filament bulb, there was a very real danger that some unscrupulous rival might steal his magic and reach the Patent Office first.

However, these same cautious moneymen were restless because of the long delay. Forgetting that other inventors had spent nearly three-quarters of a century on these problems without success, they begrudged Edison the fifteen months it had taken him to produce a practical electric bulb. They wanted proof of success and they wanted publicity. Thus, in effect, they were asking Edison not only to keep his invention completely secret, but to make it swiftly public.

Aware of this pressure from Wall Street, Edison thoughtfully trod unlighted Christie Street from home to laboratory and from laboratory to home— usually in the silence of the night. The windows of Sally Jordan's boardinghouse, and of the homes of Batchelor, Kruesi, and others were dark, or were illuminated only by dim kerosene lamps. Like most of the other streets on the planet, this short thoroughfare was pitch-black all night long, save in the brighter phases of the moon. Walking through that darkness, Edison dreamed of the time when this street and all others would be safely lighted, and when cheerful electric illumination would also shine from almost every window in the world.

Caught between the seemingly contradictory demands of the financiers, Edison took at least one precaution. Remembering his talented friend Marshall Fox, star reporter of the New York *Herald,* he asked him to come to Menlo Park with a good newspaper artist. In view of the many unfriendly, critical, and poorly informed articles which were now jibing at

Edison's Electric Light
Each of the features of the light shown
represented one or more Edison patents.

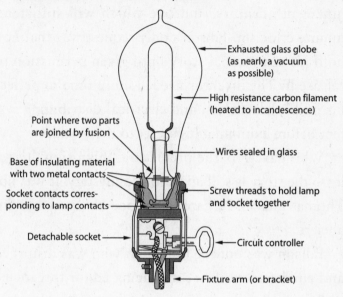

Exhausted glass globe
(as nearly a vacuum
as possible)

High resistance carbon filament
(heated to incandescence)

Point where two parts
are joined by fusion

Wires sealed in glass

Base of insulating material
with two metal contacts

Socket contacts corres-
ponding to lamp contacts

Screw threads to hold lamp
and socket together

Detachable socket

Circuit controller

Fixture arm (or bracket)

Edison's failure, the inventor wanted at least one ac-
curate feature story, ready to be released at the proper
moment. With good reason Edison believed that Fox
could write such an article.

For two weeks the reporter and his artist prowled
the laboratory, gathering data. They were given every
possible aid from Edison and all of his top assistants.
No restrictions were placed upon their coverage
of this great news scoop, and Upton helped revise

the copy to assure scientific accuracy. The result was one of the most significant scientific articles of the nineteenth century, and one which will still stand minute criticism. Edison's only request was that Fox hold his sensational story until given permission to release it. The inventor needed more time to perfect his bulbs, generators, and electrical distributing system before exhibiting his secret to the world.

Who gave Fox the premature "high sign" to release the story is still an unsolved mystery. It was not Thomas Edison. Perhaps it was one of the restless financiers.

Edison was not the only man who was disturbed and embarrassed. Fox's managing editor threatened to fire his star reporter for printing such a "preposterous" story. Glowing lights hanging from a wire? The *Herald* would be the laughingstock of the whole country. Fortunately Fox was not fired. But his news story, and others which followed, forced Edison and his staff to work like inspired beavers to produce the miracle promised—a New Year's Eve demonstration of electrical illumination at Menlo Park.

Night and day during the last week of 1879, the laboratory manufactured cardboard filament bulbs, strung lights along Christie Street, and wired the laboratory, library, machine shop and Mrs. Jordan's boardinghouse.

Although the demonstration was scheduled for New Year's Eve, the newspaper publicity brought an immediate influx of journalists and curious laymen who could not be turned away. As the news items continued to appear, the pressure was so great that the Pennsylvania Railroad put on special trains to carry the heavy traffic to that tiny depot.

Stories running in the *Herald* dramatized the comradeship of the laboratory and the essential democracy of Edison himself. "Edison animates the men and boys—there is scarcely a gray head in the establishment—with his own indomitable, persistent spirit . . . The truth is, Edison attracts the right kind of people . . . It is not a mere day's work that he exacts from them or himself."

The *Herald* reporter, together with Edison and his foremost assistants, stayed at the laboratory all day and most of the night. Sometimes the men gathered around the organ to sing a parody of *Pinafore* in honor of their chief:

> "*I am the Wizard of electric light,*
> *And a wide-awake Wizard, too . . .*"

Then the organist—a man named MacGregor—switched to Strauss and later Offenbach. Finally the glass blower was asked to play his zither. Boehm blushed with pleasure and began a quaint German serenade, "Something of dreamy moonlight on the Rhine in the tinkling treble and the moaning bass strings."

Just outside this enchanted group, other men worked at the furnace, carbonized filaments, operated the mercury pumps, or asked the eternal question, "When do we eat?" Young Jehl in particular was hungry; in fact he was always hungry.

Edison, in a crumpled felt hat, with a white silk handkerchief around his throat, his vest half buttoned, requested his favorite song, "The Heart Bowed Down." Then he sent Francis to rustle up some food. Until dawn tinted the windows they worked, sang, ate, argued science, or napped on the benches. Everyone, including the *Herald* reporter, felt lifted above the monotony of daily life. They were tired, but they were unaccountably happy.

At last the great night itself arrived. Once again the best record of the event is to be found in the New York *Herald*:

Edison's laboratory was tonight thrown open to the general public for the inspection of his electric light. Extra trains were run from east and west, and notwithstanding the stormy weather, hundreds of persons availed themselves of the privilege. The laboratory was brilliantly illuminated with twenty-five electric lamps, the office and counting room with eight, and twenty others were distributed in the street leading to the depot and in some of the adjoining houses.

Christie Street was no longer dark. Street lights gleamed upon the new-fallen snow as happy crowds of visitors climbed the hill from the depot, saying "marvelous," "beyond belief."

Edison and his associates explained in detail the entire system, answered hundreds of questions. One demonstration consisted of placing a light bulb under water to show that this in no way affected its performance. Lights were swiftly switched on and off with a "screw" to prove that this did not destroy the filament. A sewing machine was operated with one of Mr. Edison's new electric motors.

The faces of the visitors glowed from the winter wind. Their eyes glowed with the excitement of the wonders they were beholding. City folks from New York and Philadelphia, farmers and their wives, fellow scientists and inventors all mingled happily in that first village of the world to be lighted with incandescent lamps.

Most of the crowd behaved extremely well, although a few meddled with equipment they were not supposed to touch. A valuable mercury pump was broken and several precious bulbs were stolen. Spectators were warned not to approach the generators too closely. No serious accidents were reported, but one incautious young woman who stooped to tie her shoelace, felt the hairpins pulled from her tresses by the magnetic force of the generators. These pins flew through the air like bees seeking honey, to cling to the poles of the big electromagnets.

Almost without exception Edison's guests considered his electric light a complete success, in fact the eighth wonder of the world. Edison himself was something of a surprise to those who had not previously seen him. He was not in dress clothes, but in his usual working garments. He appealed to the crowd as a singularly modest young man, but definitely a genius. He had given this first-night audience a dramatic glimpse into the future, when electricity, "the great burden bearer," would lighten the work of all humanity, and would throw its mellow gleam across the darkness which had encompassed the earth at night since the beginning of the world.

When midnight struck on that New Year's Eve there were still visitors lingering in the lighted village, reluctant to leave. And when the joyous midnight bells of Metuchen, Rahway, and all the other nearby towns came pealing through the frosty air, they seemed to proclaim not only the birth of a new year and a new decade, but the birth of an entirely new era—the era of the electric light.

7

THE NEXT
HALF CENTURY

"I never allow myself to become discouraged."
Thomas A. Edison

Edison had created an electric lamp, but the task of lighting the world had scarcely begun. He must now invent electric meters, plugs, fuses, switches, and efficient generators. He must design a completely new, safe, and much more economical method for distributing electricity. In fact, the job ahead of him was so staggering that it would have discouraged almost any man except Edison.

During the 1880's the inventor's brain glowed like one of his own incandescent bulbs. In an amazingly short time he had patented some 360 electrical inventions, several of utmost importance.

While still maintaining part of his staff at Menlo Park, Edison moved his business headquarters to 65 Fifth Avenue, New York City. A handsome old residence was converted into luxurious offices. Here

Edison could display his electrical equipment, and also entertain visiting scientists, financiers, and other important men. From his Fifth Avenue office, his activities spread outward like rays of light.

For instance, he was manufacturing light bulbs, first in Menlo Park, then in Harrison, New Jersey. At Menlo Park he was happily experimenting with an electric train that sped over nearly three miles of uneven track and around dangerous curves. At Goerck Street in New York City he operated a big machine shop where he was perfecting his new dynamos. Meanwhile he also amused himself by planning to manufacture dolls that could talk or sing in any language (with the aid of the tiny phonographs inside them).

During these years he spent more than $100,000 sending courageous explorers all over Asia, South America, and Africa in search of various kinds of bamboo and other possible fibers for lamp filaments. An entire book could be written about their harrowing adventures. The best bamboo was found in Japan and put into use while luckless explorers in other regions were still struggling through the jungles, unaware that the search had ended.

Although Edison was too busy personally to

attend the Electrical Exhibition in Paris in 1881, he sent a twenty-seven-ton generator and enough equipment to light a large exhibit space. His lights proved to be so much superior to those of all his competitors that he was voted the Diploma of Honor, the highest possible award. This surprised and pleased Edison, who for so many years had faced criticism and even scorn from certain scientists and rival inventors. Some of his critics now cabled their congratulations and apologies.

Edison, however, had little time to enjoy his new honors. He was struggling to install six "Jumbo" dynamos in an old building on Pearl Street in New York City's financial district. He was also beginning the tremendous undertaking of digging trenches and burying electric cables in streets serving several square blocks to that area. Edison himself was often to be seen deep in those ditches, directing the work both by day and by night.

On September 4, 1882, the first of the Pearl Street dynamos was put in operation, lighting the building of the New York *Herald* and many others near it. To celebrate the new era of light, the inventor staged a spectacular electrical parade on Broadway. Each of the marchers had a gleaming electric globe on his cap, supplied with current from a generator powered by a fire engine. It took superb marching, daring horsemanship and clever engineering to keep that glistening parade alight and unelectrocuted.

News of Edison's successes spread rapidly. Soon letters were coming in from all over the nation and the world. Financiers were eager to lease the patent rights, to incorporate other lighting companies. A maze of corporations grew up around Edison, until even his great brain sometimes became bewildered with the endless business complications.

No wonder that after a few years of such bustling confusion he was willing to sell out most of his business interests to a corporation which soon would become the General Electric Company of Schenectady, New York. Edison knew what he wanted, it was what he had always wanted: a good laboratory and the time to do his scientific research and inventing. Once again his mind turned toward the peaceful New Jersey hills—this time the well-forested Orange Mountains.

Edison's life is generally told as one long success story. He is usually pictured as endlessly cheerful and never downhearted. While he certainly was one of the most courageous and determined citizens who ever benefited his country, he had many near-disasters, his share of sickness and numerous private sorrows. Several times he was nearly wiped out by fire. A trusted attorney stole a whole sheaf of his valuable inventions. Edison never brought legal action against this old friend. Litigation on other matters, however, took countless months of his precious time. For years his finances were precarious (although he was a better businessman than most people realize).

One of his greatest misfortunes at about this time was the loss of his beloved wife, the pretty Mary Stilwell, who had worked beside him in the old Newark days, and who had borne him the three children who romped on the lawn at Menlo Park. When Mary died in 1884, Thomas Edison was left alone and sad. In that year Marion, Thomas Alva, Jr., and William, were eleven, eight, and six—far too young to be left motherless. Menlo Park, where he had been so happy with Mary, lost the last of its attractions. He closed his laboratory on the hilltop, hoping never to return.

It must be remembered that Edison packed twenty

busy hours into almost every day of his life, and crowded many years into every calendar year. Some two years and many lonely midnights after he had lost Mary, he began to fall in love with Mina Miller, the beautiful daughter of an Akron, Ohio, inventor and manufacturer.

Thomas and Mina were married in Akron. Soon they set up housekeeping in a many-chimneyed mansion in Llewellyn Park, New Jersey, not far from the site Edison had chosen for his new laboratory. Here at "Glenmont" they could provide a gracious home for Edison's three children. And here Mina, in turn, bore the inventor three more children: Madeleine, Charles, and Theodore. During the winter the family journeyed south to Fort Myers, Florida, where in another home, surrounded by flowers, they spent the winter months. Edison had a little laboratory at his winter place. Inventing was his joy—his play as well as his work.

For more than forty years this was the pleasant pattern of their companionable lives. For Mina, who loved flowers, it was a pilgrimage from the orchids of Florida to the great laurels of New Jersey. For her husband it was a pilgrimage from one laboratory to another.

On the lower slope of a wooded hill in West Orange, New Jersey, adjoining an apple orchard, bricklayers were hard at work in the summer of 1887. They were building Edison's new laboratory, which was to be the best-equipped for industrial research in the world.

The main building, containing the vast library and office, was three stories high. From his desk in this great room, Edison could lift his eyes upward past two tiers of balconies where thousands of technical volumes rested on their shelves. Above his desk an enormous clock continuously reminded him that time is precious. From the exterior, this handsome brick structure looked more like a college administration building than a business establishment. This was doubly true as ivy climbed the walls and framed the arched windows.

Soon several other needed buildings were added. Here Edison would spend the rest of his life inventing, experimenting, and manufacturing. The boy from Port Huron at last had the sort of laboratory he had always wanted.

Today we distinguish between "pure science" and "applied science" as though no single human being could practice both branches. By pure science we mean research for its own sake with no practical application in view. By applied science we mean the use of scientific ideas to produce practical (and usually salable) objects.

Really great men can seldom be easily classified. The artist Leonardo da Vinci was both a pure and a practical scientist as well as poet, architect, and painter. Edison had a trace of the pure scientist, but was mainly an applied scientist, a technician, and a businessman. He usually tried to find a profitable use for his inventions—but this was not always true.

For instance, he never attempted to capitalize on his marvelous tasimeter, but gave this invention to mankind. The same was true of the fluoroscope, which doctors use today to view your bones and inner organs. Edison did not patent this great invention, but made a gift of it to the world.

Two other discoveries in pure science on which he labored, mostly for love, were "etheric force" and the "Edison-Effect" tube—both essential to modern radio and wireless.

Edison had noticed while experimenting with electricity that sparks were sometimes seen far from the nearest electrical contact, leaping from a gas pipe to some other metal object. Whatever these sparks were, they did not seem to be electricity as he knew it, since they could not be measured on his most sensitive galvanometer.

What he was seeing were manifestations of what we call radio waves. In time the inventor learned how to produce and control these waves so well that he could send messages from a moving train by "grasshopper telegraph" to any station which the train was passing. He could also send messages from ship to shore. This was wireless in its earliest stages and could have made Edison a fortune. But he did not follow it up. Instead he sold, for a very reasonable sum, his basic patents in this field to his friend Guglielmo Marconi, whose own contributions in this complex field were so great that he, rather than Edison, is called the "inventor" of the wireless.

In a similar way the Edison-Effect tube became the basis for the modern radio tube (later perfected by Lee De Forest), while his motograph receiver, or "shouting telephone," was the first crude "loudspeaker." Thomas Edison was also the inventor of the radio antenna. He was the almost unrecognized grandfather of electronics.

In other words, Edison frequently considered pure

knowledge more precious than mere money, and research at least as important for its own sake as for any salable end-product it might produce. Nearly half a century before Hollywood commercialized the talking picture, Edison visualized such a possibility. Even in his Menlo Park days, he realized that if his newly invented phonograph could be geared to a machine which could project several pictures a minute on a screen, then any human being's voice and appearance could be made "immortal." Thus we could see and hear an individual long after he was dead.

Upon setting up his laboratory in West Orange, Edison began to explore this exciting possibility. He knew that the eye retains an image for several moments—long enough to cover the interval it takes to shift from one picture to the next, flashed swiftly upon a screen.

At the inventor's request, George Eastman began producing long strips of film of the sort we now call "movie film." Edison rapidly perfected a method for running them through a specially designed camera called the kinetograph, then projecting them through his kinetoscope. This was the birth of motion pictures.

Some of the first movies were filmed in a tar-paper

shack at West Orange known as the "Black Maria." This strange-looking building could be turned on tracks so that bright sunshine could pour directly through a large trap door in the roof, thus giving the strong light needed for the first movie cameras. In these early films, any simple performance satisfied. A man sneezed; a Spanish dancer whirled; a trained bear shuffled through a waltz. Jim Corbett, the famous heavyweight, was hired for a short boxing film. When the unsuspecting sparring partner saw whom he was facing, he jumped over the ropes and left for parts unknown, still wearing his boxing shorts. Edison laughed over this incident for the rest of his life.

Etheric force, Edison-Effect tubes, fluoroscopes, tasimeters, the carbon telephone transmitter, the light bulb, motion pictures, the ever-improving phonograph—how can one classify their inventor except to say that whether he was a "pure" or an "applied" scientist, he was one of the great men of all time?

During the 1890's Edison's most ambitious single project was an expensive venture in mining iron. Once on a fishing trip off the shores of Long Island, Edison had noticed a beach of black sand which proved to be largely fine-grained iron ore. He soon developed a process for separating the iron from the other sand.

Like so many of his inventions, this process seems simple once it is understood. The iron-bearing sand was merely sifted past a powerful magnet. The magnet drew the iron dust to one side. The other sand, being unaffected by the magnet, fell directly to the ground. The result was a pile of sand, and a second pile of almost pure iron nearer to the magnet.

Soon one thousand tons of highly concentrated iron ore were separated from the Long Island beach. Then a storm blew up and washed the whole beach into the Atlantic. The process was a success, but now Edison must find another source of ore.

Near the village of Ogdensburg, New Jersey, a large deposit of iron ore was discovered, but it was embedded in very solid rock. The inventor was not dismayed. He designed huge rotating rock crushers, ranging downward from six feet in diameter to other rollers much smaller in size. Into the hopper of those crushers went giant boulders, which sometimes bounced thirty feet into the air. The noise was terrific as these chunks of the hillside were pulverized to powder, run through the magnetic separator, mixed

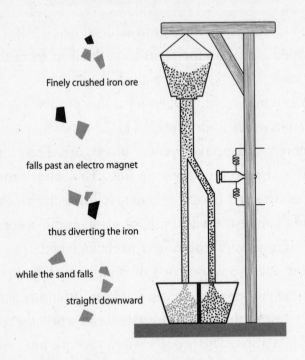

Finely crushed iron ore

falls past an electro magnet

thus diverting the iron

while the sand falls

straight downward

Edison's invention for separating iron ore

with resin and baked into briquettes. The inventor poured nearly $2,000,000 and some ten years of his life into this business enterprise. Then additional rich and easily worked iron mines were discovered in the Great Lakes region. Edison's expensive process could not meet this new competition. He approached financial ruin.

At about this time his associate W. S. Mallory, manager of the mine, had another major worry. His beloved daughter Charlotte lay near death from a badly injured knee. Infection was spreading all through her body. If it were not for the ninety-seven-degree heat she might have a chance to recover, but the heat wave showed no sign of breaking.

"We'll change the weather," Edison promised.

Ignoring the tremendous financial loss at the closed mine, Edison began concentrating on his new problem, Charlotte's health. He brought hammer, nails, a wooden box, large chunks of ice, and one of his own electric fans to Charlotte's room. Soon he had constructed an "air-conditioning machine" in her window. The fan blew air across the ice, cooling the room by more than ten degrees. For the first time in days the child seemed to relax and sleep more normally.

Charlotte finally passed her crisis, but she was still pale and weak.

"What she needs is a trip to the mountains or the seashore," the doctor said. "She would mend more quickly there."

However, Charlotte was too tired and listless to be moved, so Edison once again came to the rescue. In his laboratory he began mixing chemicals, sniffing each new concoction until he was quite satisfied. He put the little bottles in his pocket and went to the Mallory residence.

"How would you like a vacation?" Edison asked. "A little trip?"

"Oh yes, please!" Charlotte said. "That would be lovely."

"Where would you like to go?"

"To the mountains, under the big pine trees."

"Very well," said Edison, "shut your eyes, Charlotte, and we'll go to the mountains." He poured several drops of liquid from one of the small bottles on the ice in front of the electric fan. In another moment the entire room was filled with the fragrance of pine trees, cool and fresh and spicy, with just a tang of woodsmoke as though from a campfire. After this trip to the mountains, Edison gave Charlotte a trip to the seashore from another little bottle. Now she could smell the salt sea wind and imagine the surf beating against the shore.

Each day Edison had some new delight for Charlotte, and soon she was up and walking again. The Mallory family always gave Edison credit for saving Charlotte's life.

Saving Edison's lost fortune was a more difficult matter. The inventor had invested almost all of his money in the iron mine. Now the mine's only asset was its machinery—the big rock crushers standing useless and rusting, exposed to the weather.

Once again Edison plunged bravely into a new venture. He designed, then redesigned, a huge cement plant at another small town in New Jersey. The rock-crushing machinery was moved and began crushing blocks of limestone for the cement kilns—the longest rotating kilns anywhere in the world. Slowly this business prospered, and Edison and Mallory began to recoup some of the fortune lost in the iron mine. There was a vein as hard as iron or cement in Edison, but a vein of tenderness, too.

The man who could invent talking dolls, or furnish artificial vacations for sick little girls, was not light-hearted all of the time, however. He had a large pay-roll to meet both at his cement factory and at his West Orange laboratories. In those days there was no great charitable foundation (or government subsidy) to underwrite research work. Edison was an individualist, very much on his own when it came to financing his long-term projects. This took patience and courage.

For instance, between 1900 and 1910 Thomas Edison worked with determination to invent a new storage battery, avoiding the usual corrosive acid between the electrodes. This alkaline storage battery was one of the most difficult problems Edison ever tackled. It must have a long life, great economy of operation, and a substance in the cells which would not attack or coat the metals of the two poles.

In five years of ceaseless effort, Edison produced a battery which would satisfy most of his customers. But it was not perfect! So he withdrew it from the market, and continued his investigation. During that decade he performed 50,000 separate experiments on the battery alone.

Night and day he labored in his laboratory. He punched the time clock as did his employees, but he more than doubled their average work week, sometimes devoting as much as 116 hours between Sunday and Sunday.

One morning a chemist on his staff came upon the now white-haired inventor, smiling with contentment after his night of labor. Edison had just completed a cycle of several hundred experiments on the battery, and the chemist misinterpreted his smile.

"You've found it!" this assistant shouted.

"No," said Edison, "but I've learned something important. I've learned that none of these things work."

"Then why are you smiling so happily?"

"Because I now can start all over again," Edison said serenely; and with perfect composure he began new weeks, and months, and years of experiments on his battery.

In time Edison was rewarded with success. He found that nickel flake more gossamer than cobweb increased the conductivity of the positive electrode. And to this day these batteries are used for railroad signal lights, and wherever else a storage battery of superior quality must serve dependably over long periods of time.

To a man like Edison, perfection was its own reward. Just as he scoured the earth for the best fibers for his lamp and spent ten years to invent and improve his battery, he now brought similar energy and high critical standards to his perfection of the phonograph and motion pictures. Years before any modern "high fidelity" enthusiast ever tinkered with his record player, Edison was at work on both high fidelity and the long-playing record. Despite his impaired hearing he was able to detect the slightest flaw in any recording or musical performance. With a

Edison Home Phonograph

pencil held between his teeth and resting on the phonograph he could "hear" a false note with unerring regularity. Recordings by even the greatest opera stars or pianists were rejected by Edison if they contained the slightest flaw. Meanwhile, he continued to improve his techniques for making motion pictures.

As early as 1913 Edison produced a talking picture. But the movie czars of that primitive era were not ready for this startling change. A decade and a half later the "talkies" revolutionized the entire industry. However, by this time most Americans had forgotten (if they ever knew) that the invention was Edison's, and that the basic idea dated back nearly half a century.

From all of these patents, as from the electric light, other businessmen made more money than did Edison. His major reward was the knowledge that he had perfected inventions which would benefit all mankind for countless generations.

Edison hated war. He said: "Making things that kill men is against my fiber." However, when the Germans invaded Belgium in 1914, and when later they began unrestricted submarine warfare against ships attempting to cross the Atlantic, Edison, as a patriotic American citizen, was deeply concerned.

Even before America entered World War I, our country was seriously endangered by the sea struggle between England and Germany. England's blockade of German freighters cut us off from many chemicals we had previously imported from Germany. One of these was carbolic acid, which Edison was using at the rate of about one and one-half tons a day in the manufacture of his disk phonograph records.

Edison, of course, was not the only American industrialist needing carbolic acid. Hundreds of other firms were desperate for this substance. Obviously a local source of supply must be created immediately.

At his West Orange laboratory Edison worked three days and nights on the problem of synthetically creating carbolic acid. Then he called in the leading manufacturing chemists. These men told him that it would take at least six months to start producing this essential acid. Edison's reply was that he would build a plant himself. Within exactly seventeen days the plant was built, the process established, and carbolic acid was being synthesized—in quantity.

When, in the spring of 1917, America could no longer endure Germany's submarine warfare and other insults to our sovereignty, we declared war. Thereupon the Navy asked Edison for scientific help in combating the submarine menace. Dropping all his other work, and serving his country without pay, Edison devised some forty defensive inventions, mostly created to counter the submarine. For this he was awarded the Distinguished Service Medal, never before presented by the Navy to any civilian.

After the war, Edison began to "relax," sometimes allowing himself six or seven hours of sleep. With his friends John Burroughs, the naturalist, Henry Ford, the automobile manufacturer, and Harvey Firestone, the rubber magnate, he took an annual tour about the country. These famous vagabonds enjoyed playing Boy Scout. They wore old clothes, slept in tents, cooked their own meals over a campfire, and tried, without much success, to avoid publicity. Almost too late Edison was trying to recapture the carefree pleasures of boyhood—joys he had seldom experienced in his youth.

We have said that Edison's work was his play, and his play was his work. We might also add that he was as determined about the one as about the other. The story is told of a fishing trip on the Atlantic when the fish were not biting. The boat was anchored for two days and two nights without so much as a nibble on any line. Grimly determined to master the nonbiting fish as he mastered all other problems, Edison refused to leave until his friends began to worry about their wives and absolutely insisted upon lifting the anchor. Still grumbling, Edison reluctantly consented, making mental reservations, however, that someday he would return to this very spot and *make* the fish bite.

He was an interesting and sometimes unpredictable man: a great reader of the classics, he was not always completely grammatical in his letters or in his speech; a kindly man, he could be very biting and gruff when displeased; a brilliant individual, he nevertheless preferred the childish game of Parcheesi to the intellectual game of chess. The *New York Times* early in the 1920's estimated that Edison had added more than fifteen billion dollars to America's wealth. Yet he had retained but a minute fraction of this wealth for himself.

Endlessly curious about the universe in which he lived, Edison took up botany at the age of eighty, and was as patient as his friend Luther Burbank in growing and crossing plants (this time in search of rubber). Edison tested more than 17,000 plants in his final years, eventually producing a strain of goldenrod rich in rubber which he felt certain would see America through any future war, should foreign supplies of rubber suddenly be denied. Had America not found a way to synthesize rubber during World War II, we undoubtedly would have grown hundreds of thousands of acres of the Edison strain of goldenrod —his final free contribution to his country's safety and welfare.

8

LIGHT'S
GOLDEN JUBILEE

"If our work has widened the horizon of man's
understanding and given even a little measure of
happiness in this world, I am content."

Thomas A. Edison

In October, 1929—the month of the great stock market crash—at least one industrialist had something more pleasant to think about. For several years Henry Ford had been planning a tribute to his friend Edison. Now Ford's project was complete and the automobile manufacturer only awaited the arrival of Edison to show him a faithful reconstruction of the Menlo Park laboratory in Greenfield Village at Dearborn, Michigan.

Greenfield Village, as most Americans know, consists of historic American houses and other buildings which were moved, board by board, and brick by brick, from their original sites to become part of this permanent exhibit of America's past. Henry Ford was grateful to Edison for the early encouragement the inventor had given him when he was struggling to build his first automobile. In addition, Ford was Edison's great admirer. How better could he express both his gratitude and his admiration than to reconstruct the Menlo Park buildings?

There was another reason for Edison's journey westward to Dearborn in October, 1929. On the twenty-first of that month the entire world was celebrating Light's Golden Jubilee, the fiftieth anniversary of the first successful incandescent bulb. At the very center of that celebration was a banquet planned by Ford for Thomas A. Edison. The guests were to include scores of the most famous men and women alive, including the President of the United States.

As Edison rolled westward over the clicking rails, every state through which he passed brought back personal memories. Not a city or village through which the train moved but had been altered by his inventions. Electric utility companies using his patents served each of these communities. His phonographs made music, his motion pictures gave pleasure and his light bulbs shed brilliance not only throughout his own country, but throughout the world. Several public opinion polls had named him the greatest living American citizen.

Sometimes the old inventor became almost weary of his honors. He had been made an Italian count. Three times he had been awarded the Legion of Honor. So frequently was his work interrupted by the arrival of dignitaries with citations and awards that Edison was sometimes amused, sometimes impatient. Asked by one such foreign ambassador of good will if he had ever previously received a medal, Edison smiled pleasantly and quipped "quarts of them." Just one year previously the Congressional Medal of Honor had been awarded, bearing his portrait and the inscription, "He illuminated the path of progress by his inventions."

Ahead of him, however, lay honors more impressive and unusual than any he had previously received. Some of them would prove a complete and delightful surprise.

For instance, at a certain station in Michigan, Edison and his party were told that here they must change cars. To his amazement the inventor found himself boarding a perfect replica of the old mixed train on which he had sold papers and peanuts as a boy. Somewhere Henry Ford had found a wood-burning locomotive exactly like the one Edison had piloted on that evening long ago—its brasswork shining, blue smoke from the big stack puffing contentedly. The highly varnished cars were authentic too, exactly as Edison remembered them some seventy years before.

Henry Ford's finest surprise however, was the baggage car. He led his old friend forward through the train to—could it be?—the exact duplicate of the train boy's rolling laboratory, complete with the racks of chemicals and all the apparatus. There too Edison found his old printing press, or one just like it, with type set up to print an issue of the *Herald*.

Edison and his host Henry Ford were as happy as small boys. The old inventor immediately began running off a few copies of the paper. Then he spied his train-butcher's apron and a basket well filled with candy, nuts, fruit, and periodicals. Putting on the apron, Edison went through the cars calling his wares and selling them to the distinguished fellow passengers.

When the engineer of this fabulous old train began to apply the brakes, Edison looked from the window, slightly bewildered. Would miracles never cease? They seemed to be pulling into the Smith's Creek depot where "Al" had been so sternly ejected after the phosphorus fire in the baggage car. But Smith's Creek as Edison well knew, was many miles away. Henry Ford laughed happily at Edison's amazement. He had purchased the old station and moved it to Greenfield Village just to surprise and please his friend.

When, two days later, this whole performance was re-enacted for the President of the United States and his party, it was Herbert Hoover who assisted Edison to the Smith's Creek platform—that same platform on which he had been tossed so roughly by the angry conductor long ago.

But Edison "hadn't seen anything yet." In Greenfield Village Henry Ford took him to Christie Street complete with the lamp posts and primitive light bulbs of fifty years ago. On Edison's right as he walked northward was Aunt Sally Jordan's boardinghouse, and ahead of him a most familiar sight, the Menlo Park laboratory and all the buildings surrounding it, perfect to the last detail.

Edison stopped and squinted at the red soil over

which he was walking. Yes, it was the same New Jersey clay. Ford had even scraped the Menlo Park hilltop to bring the very earth to Greenfield Village.

Stepping through the gate in the picket fence, Edison noticed that each building was exactly as he remembered it, the office and library, the machine shop, even the smoky carbon shed and the little glass blower's house. The stump of the hickory tree where the bear had once been chained stood in its proper place. And there at the door of the laboratory stood Francis Jehl, the Sorcerer's Apprentice, nearing seventy now, but ready to serve his old employer. For years he had been a utility executive in Europe. Now, however, he was pleasantly engaged as curator of the Edison museum buildings in Greenfield Village.

"Hello, Francis," Edison cried happily, as Jehl hastened toward him.

To the very last item the laboratory was precisely as Edison recalled it: every chemical, every instrument, every fiber for a filament! As they climbed to the second floor, Edison's lips quivered "with a prolonged, silent 'Aaa-hhh—!'" Even the pipe organ was in its proper place.

"It is 99.9 per cent perfect," Edison said at last.

"And the last tenth of one per cent?" Ford asked.

"Our floor was never so clean."

Now Jehl once again became Edison's apprentice as they went to work making a cotton-thread light globe. The proper thread was at hand, as was the little furnace in which to carbonize it. At eighty-two the inventor's fingers had not lost their delicate magic, nor had Francis Jehl forgotten how to use the mercury pumps for creating a vacuum in the globe. As in the old days, Jehl had to climb a stepladder to operate the pump, carrying twenty-pound containers of mercury; but he was fifty years older, which made the task difficult. Edison feared that Jehl might slip and suggested that he put sand on the steps of the ladder. Happily these two old friends, the Wizard of Menlo Park and his assistant, labored to process a bulb almost to its completion—the final phase to be saved for a public occasion on Light's Golden Jubilee.

Every civilized nation in the world joined in the celebration of Light's Golden Jubilee. On October 21, 1929, the festival of lights began in the Far East—in Japan, China, and Java—and slowly encircled the globe. Dusk on every continent was the signal for a myriad of lights that blossomed like luminous flowers. Electric towers and arches, fountains and gardens thrust back the dark. Never before or since has an inventor been so universally honored.

At the Edison Institute in Dearborn (a large and handsome building erected by Henry Ford), the banquet hall was lighted with candles in memory of the dim world previous to Edison's invention. Here were gathered nearly 500 of the world's most notable citizens. Perhaps the most distinguished of all was the frail Madame Curie, co-discoverer of radium, who had made the transatlantic crossing for this event. Here too were Herbert Hoover, President of the United States, Henry Ford, host at this banquet, and others equally famous. Owen D. Young of General Electric was the toastmaster, and he managed to keep the pace of the many tributes swift enough to please even the millions of radio listeners.

Most formal banquets need an intermission—but few have one. This affair had a carefully planned dramatic interlude. Edison, Hoover, Ford, and Jehl excused themselves and left, through the darkness and rain, for the Menlo Park laboratory, where the light bulb attached to the vacuum pump was swiftly completed, sealed and lighted. All the radio listeners, including those at the dinner, could follow this process step by step.

When the guests of honor returned, the candle-lit banquet hall suddenly gleamed with hundreds of electric lights in recognition of the fact that Edison and his loyal assistant had again performed the miracle.

Although he had invented some of the component parts of the radio, including the microphone, Edison was always "mike shy." He dreaded the ordeal of speaking over the microphone, but he was determined to do his duty. The venerable white-haired figure now arose before the hushed assemblage. Possibly only his wife, remembering his recent illness, realized the courage he was displaying:

> I am told that tonight my voice will reach out to the four corners of the world . . . I would be embarrassed at the honors that are being heaped upon me on this unforgettable night, were it not for the fact that in honoring me you are also honoring that vast army of thinkers and workers . . . without whom my work would have gone for nothing . . . If our work has widened the horizon of man's understanding and given even a little measure of happiness in this world, I am content.

Mina Edison had noticed that her husband was near to collapse. As he sank to his chair she quietly summoned help from those around her. Edison was half carried to a room near the banquet hall, where President Hoover's own physician aided the stricken man. After a time he began to show signs of recovery.

"It was nothing but stage fright, Francis," he said to his worried assistant.

The greatly honored inventor lived for two more years after this memorable evening (when so many million lamps glowed through the rain and the mist). He died, as all mortals must, but the powerful dynamo of his mind, moving more slowly now, did not completely forsake him. Thinking was still his greatest pleasure. He had lived a partial doubter. But in his last conscious moment he turned to his wife and said, "It's very beautiful over there."

THE EDISON
HISTORICAL SITES

The most important historic sites and buildings connected with Thomas A. Edison have fortunately been preserved and are open to visitors at stated times or by advance arrangement. In these may be found a wealth of material objects, as well as rich sources of inspiration, dealing with Edison's life and work. Please visit each site's Web site for further information.

EDISON BIRTHPLACE MUSEUM, Milan, Ohio. Administered by the Edison Birthplace Association. Here is the modest brick cottage where Edison was born and lived until his family moved to Port Huron, Michigan. The house is appropriately furnished. www.tom edison.org

MENLO PARK MUSEUM, Edison Township, New Jersey. Site of the inventor's Menlo Park laboratory. The concrete tower, 131 feet high, marks the spot where the first practical incandescent lamp was made and tested in 1879. www.menloparkmuseum.com

HENRY FORD MUSEUM AND GREENFIELD VILLAGE, Dearborn, Michigan. The museum proper contains exhibits connected with Edison's work in electric lighting and other technical fields. In Greenfield Village are many of the old Menlo Park buildings, moved here from their original location, and now faithfully restored. www.hfmgv.org

EDISON LABORATORY NATIONAL MONUMENT, West Orange, New Jersey. Administered by the National Park Service, United States Department of the Interior. Includes the library, chemical laboratory, and workshops of Edison erected in 1887 and used by him until his death in 1931. Many originals or replicas of his inventions are on display. Here also is a reconstruction of "Black Maria," the first motion picture studio in the world, where old Edison films are shown regularly. www.nps.gov

EDISON NATIONAL HISTORIC SITE, West Orange, New Jersey. Administered by the National Park Service, United States Department of the Interior. This beautiful estate, familiarly known as "Glenmont," is preserved as the principal Edison family residence from 1886 to 1931. In the library over the entranceway

Edison developed many ideas which later took shape at his laboratory in the valley below. www.nps.gov

EDISON & FORD WINTER ESTATES, Fort Myers, Florida. Owned by the City of Fort Myers. Includes Edison's winter residence, laboratories, and thirteen-acre botanical garden, where he developed improved strains of goldenrod for the extraction of natural rubber. www.efwefla.org

INDEX

TURN THE PAGE FOR AN EXCERPT FROM
ANOTHER STERLING NORTH BIOGRAPHY

MARK TWAIN

~AND THE RIVER~

⌒ 1 ⌒
A FRONTIER PARADISE
(1835–1844)

Uncle John Quarles stepped down from his farm wagon and tied his team to the hitching post in front of the modest frame house on Hill Street. He noticed that the new home had been given a coat of white paint, and that the shutters on the five front windows were a gleaming dark green. Even the fence had a fresh coat of whitewash.

Quarles smiled with pleasure. His brother-in-law "Judge" Clemens, that proud but unsuccessful tradesman and lawyer, was apparently beginning to pull himself out of debt.

Uncle John wondered which of her children Jane Clemens had dragooned into whitewashing that fence. Certainly not the oldest son, Orion, who at eighteen spent most of his time in St. Louis learning the printing trade. Pamela at sixteen was a gentle young lady with musical inclinations—and no young lady in Hannibal, Missouri, in the year 1844 would be asked to sully her hands with a job like whitewashing a fence. Henry at six was a very good boy, but too young for such a task. So it must have been that rascal Sam, whose eight and a half years had been crammed with more mischief than useful labor. Uncle John liked Sammy the best of all, with his "ruck" of russet curls and his merry blue-green eyes, the delight and despair of his sprightly mother, Jane.

John Quarles had come to Hannibal on the previous afternoon. Not wishing to crowd the little Clemens home, he had spent the night at a neighboring hotel. Now that he had made his purchases, he was ready to pick up Jane and Sam for their summerlong holiday at the big Quarles farm near Florida, Missouri. Aunt "Patsy" Quarles was Jane's sister, and throughout the summer they buzzed away at each other, happy as bees in clover.

For a moment Uncle John paused to view the little white town of Hannibal, bathed in the misty sunlight of this June morning. The village lay cupped in a valley between bluffs to the north and the south. All its attention was centered on the mighty Mississippi, which carried, on its flowing tide, rafts of white pine lumber, handsome side-wheel steamers, painted and gilded; and in flood times masses of floating driftwood and even cabins washed from their foundations. This brown and swirling highway to distant New Orleans captured the imagination of any man who looked upon it—a dangerous river, a beautiful river draining most of the American continent. John Quarles did not wonder that his nephew, little Sammy Clemens, and all the other barefooted boys of Hannibal, were constantly risking their lives in or on its waters.

It would be a long, dusty drive, that thirty-five winding miles to the farm, and this day looked as though it might be another sizzler; so Uncle John turned his gaze from the river to the front door of the house, open for summer coolness, and garlanded on the step with several drowsing cats.

"Jane!" he boomed heartily. "Sam! . . . Where is everybody? Time to get going!"

Sam Clemens, sitting comfortably between his mother and his uncle John on the wide seat of the farm wagon, watched the team of dapple-grays flicking flies with their tails as they ambled easily along the road. He didn't know whether to be happy as a meadow lark or sad as a whippoorwill as the wheels rumbled along the rutted trail leading westward from Hannibal.

It was one of those almost impossible choices which a boy must always be making, such as whether to play Robin Hood or whether to play Pirate; whether to let your warts grow, or whether to risk your life trying to cure them with spunk-water to be found in old hollow stumps in the middle of haunted woods at midnight during the dark of the moon.

Every summer he had to make the same difficult decision about his vacation: whether to stay in Hannibal with Pamela and Henry, and his father the "Judge"—or go with his mother to the Quarles farm. It was always hard to say good-bye to his best friends, Will Bowen, John Briggs, and that happy-go-lucky vagabond, Tom Blankenship, who never had to go to school, and who spent a perfectly heavenly life sleeping in barrels, smoking a corncob pipe, and doing anything else he pleased. But the farm was a gay and joyous place too.

Back in Hannibal he could always go swimming in Bear Creek and risk getting drowned for the ninth time, or fish catfish, or visit the big cave, which went forever and ever in mysterious passages. But at the farm there was at least a cool creek to wade in and swings that went so high in the air that a tumble sometimes meant a broken bone. That was almost as exciting as nearly getting drowned.

There were girls, of course, at both places: little Laura Hawkins, his best girl, lived just across the street in Hannibal; once he had given her his finest possession, a shining brass knob from the top of an andiron. But she would probably wait for him faithfully until he returned in the autumn. At the farm was his gay little cousin, Tabitha Quarles, answering to the name of "Puss." Sam wasn't in love with Puss, he just liked her, and they had happy and silly times together. In a way that was much more comfortable than being in love. So in the girl department, the two places just about balanced off.

Girls, however, mattered only part of the time. Boy companions and the storytelling slaves were what made things lively; and there were plenty of each at both places. In fact there were eight cousins and more than twenty slaves at the Quarles farm, making life as wonderful there as it was in Hannibal.

It was probably the delicious meals Aunt Patsy always served which tipped the scales in favor of another summer at the farm: "Fried chicken, roast pig; wild and tame turkeys, ducks and geese; venison just killed; squirrels, rabbits, pheasants, partridges, prairie chickens; biscuits, hot batter cakes, hot wheat bread, hot rolls, hot corn pone; fresh corn boiled on the ear, succotash, butter beans . . . watermelons, muskmelons, cantaloupes—all fresh from the garden; apple pie, peach pie, pumpkin pie, apple dumplings . . ." Sam couldn't even remember all the rest, but it made him "mouth-watering hungry" just to think of all that good food.

Yes, going to the farm again this summer was an excellent idea, Sam Clemens finally decided as they wound westward and ever westward through the hills of Missouri on that June morning so long ago.

Westward and ever westward might have been the marching cry of the entire nation during the nineteenth century. Like hundreds of thousands of other pioneers, Sam Clemens' father and mother had felt that urge early and often.

John Marshall Clemens, who came of Virginia stock, was reared in Kentucky. Fatherless from the age of seven, and entirely self-supporting from his fourteenth year, he studied for the law, and, being a young man of "honesty, probity and good demeanor," was soon licensed to practice. Although he had worked hard with his hands during his youth, and throughout life was haunted by fear of poverty, he considered himself quite rightly a gentleman and a scholar. He was proud, just, austere, idealistic, dyspeptic, and so lacking in outward signs of affection that Sam never saw him kiss wife or child, save in the presence of death.

Two more strikingly different people than Sam's father and mother could scarcely be imagined.

Jane Lampton (Clemens), whom John married in Columbia, Kentucky, on May 6th, 1823, was one of the most beautiful young women of her region and era. Her oldest son, Orion, wrote of her vivacity and charm. "To the last she retained her rosy cheeks and fine complexion. She took part in the custom in Kentucky and Tennessee, of going on horseback from house to house during the week from Christmas to New Year. To the music of one or two violins they danced all night, slept a little, ate breakfast, and danced all day at the next house . . . Even in the last year of her life she liked to show a company the beautiful step and graceful movement she had learned in her youth." She had a tart tongue but a tender heart.

There was a rumor, never quite denied by Jane, that she married John Marshall Clemens on the rebound, having been jilted by a young doctor she deeply loved. Be that as it may, she was always a good and faithful wife to her lawyer husband, carrying her heavy load cheerfully through many years of poverty. She guided her children with humor, love and flashes of temper, but always with far greater understanding than that showed by her unbending husband.

Sam respected his father; but he loved his mother, whose temperament was so like his own, and from whom he inherited his wit, his high spirits and his russet curls.

From Kentucky, John Marshall Clemens and his young wife Jane soon moved to Tennessee. They must have made a striking pair—John with his erect posture, his piercing eyes and well-cut features— tall, spare, wearing a blue swallow-tail coat with brass buttons, and the high silk hat expected of a lawyer; Jane young and lovely, with a mischievous tongue and laughing blue-gray eyes and a mass of auburn hair with gold glinting in the curls.

In the wilderness settlements on the upper reaches of the Cumberland River they were considered "Quality" by the log-cabin dwellers because, among other high-flown notions, they insisted upon plastering the inside of their new house. For a time John seemed to be prospering. As acting Attorney General he drew up plans for improving the state in a flawless "copper plate script." At about this time he purchased for the small sum of $400 seventy-five thousand acres of wild, hilly, infertile, forested Tennessee land. This was to be the legacy, the riches for coming generations. It was a rosy-tinted dream that sustained the family during years of poverty— but a dream that never came true. Hold the land! Never let it go! And the Clemens family did hold the land for a generation and a half. But Tennessee was developed so slowly, and the land was so rough and infertile, that when the vast estate slipped from their hands it brought them little more than John Marshall Clemens had paid for it so many years before.

John and Jane moved several times in Tennessee, and always downhill. Poverty came—and then greater poverty. And with the poverty came the children. First there was Orion (which they mispronounced Oh'-rean). This first-born son, who would always have stars in his eyes, and his head in the clouds, came in 1825. He was named for the most conspicuous constellation in the midnight sky—for there was always a touch of poetry in the hearts of John and Jane Clemens.

Next in line was gentle Pamela, born in 1827. She loved music from earliest childhood and would one day play the piano and the guitar. She was never any trouble to her parents and was always her father's favorite child. Years later when he lay dying he asked to kiss but one member of the family—his beloved Pamela.

Third to use the cradle was a rosy little girl named Margaret, most beautiful of all the Clemens children. She arrived with the redbud and dogwood blossoms in May, 1830.

There was a little boy named Pleasants Hannibal, who lived just three months, and then came Benjamin, last of the Tennessee children, born in June, 1832.

They were *wanted* children, loved by the mother, gently treated by the father. But how were the Clemenses to feed so many hungry mouths? John and Jane realized that they must again make a move, this time to some more prosperous region.

As though in answer to their unspoken desire for greener pastures, letters now began to arrive from a frontier settlement called Florida, Missouri—letters praising the fertile limestone soil, the towering hardwood timber, the excellent water and the abundance of game in this unspoiled region. One great attraction for Jane was the fact that so many of her Kentucky kinfolk had already moved to this Missouri village. From her sister Patsy Quarles and Patsy's husband John came affectionate letters urging the Clemenses to pull up stakes and hurry west. Soon this cluster of cabins would be a large and prospering town—or so they all fondly believed. Jane's favorite cousin, James Lampton, went so far as to claim that the shallow Salt River could be deepened and improved until the largest steamboats on the Mississippi could ascend that winding rivulet to deposit passengers and cargo at their very door.*

In the late spring of 1835, John and Jane Clemens

---

* James Lampton, always aglow with "blazing enthusiasm," was the original from whom Mark Twain portrayed his fascinating character Colonel Sellers in *The Gilded Age*. There is a vivid description in that novel of just such a family as the Clemenses moving from the hills of Tennessee to a similar frontier village in Missouri.

and their four living children, Orion, Pamela, Margaret, and Benjamin, loaded their meager possessions into a wagon and began their long journey to Florida, Missouri. Orion, and their one slave, a girl named Jennie, rode horseback. The rest of the family crowded into the wagon. With a sense of high adventure and new hope they clucked to the horses and joined the great westward movement. Somewhere along the way Jane Clemens discovered that she would bear yet another child. She could not know that the new life stirring within her was a baby who would become America's most famous and best-loved humorist. But she did know that this one, like the others, would be welcomed and suckled, loved and chided. And she had the bright hope that this newest arrival when it came into the world would have a better chance to live and thrive in the promised land toward which they were journeying.